New Hampshire

Annotated and Illustrated

Poetry by Robert Frost

Robert Frost &

Lisa Shea

Original Content copyright © 2019 by

Lisa Shea / Minerva Webworks LLC

All rights reserved

No part of this book may be reproduced in any form or by any electronic or mechanical means including information storage and retrieval systems, without permission in writing from the author. The only exception is by a reviewer, who may quote short excerpts in a review.

~ v1 ~

The original book "New Hampshire" by Robert Frost was published in 1923. It became public domain in 2019.

Contents

Introduction 8

New Hampshire 3

A Star in a Stone-Boat 19

The Census-Taker 23

The Star-Splitter 27

Maple 32

The Ax-Helve 40

The Grindstone 45

Paul's Wife 49

Wild Grapes 56

Place for a Third 61

Two Witches 66

    The Witch of Coos 66

    The Pauper Witch of Grafton 73

An Empty Threat 78

A Fountain, a Bottle, a Donkey's Ears, and Some Books 82

I Will Sing You One-O 90

Fragmentary Blue 94

Fire and Ice 96

In a Disused Graveyard.. 98

Dust of Snow.. 100

To E.T. 102

Nothing Gold Can Stay.. 104

The Runaway 106

The Aim Was Song 108

Stopping by Woods on a Snowy Evening................ 110

For Once, Then, Something 112

Blue-Butterfly Day... 114

The Onset 116

To Earthward 118

Good-by and Keep Cold 121

Two Look at Two... 124

Not to Keep 127

A Brook in the City.. 129

The Kitchen Chimney 131

Looking for a Sunset Bird in Winter....................... 133

A Boundless Moment 135

Evening in a Sugar Orchard 137

Gathering Leaves 139

The Valley's Singing Day 142

Misgiving 144

A Hillside Thaw 146

Plowmen 149

On a Tree Fallen Across the Road 151

Our Singing Strength 153

The Lockless Door 156

The Need of Being Versed in Country Things 158

Summary 161

Dedication 164

About the Author 165

Free Ebooks 166

Live Free Or Die

Introduction

I adore Robert Frost's poetry. I could quote his works all day long. I also love New Hampshire. I've lived in its near neighbor, Massachusetts, for over twenty years. I have driven the length and breadth of New Hampshire, motorcycled there, camped there, hiked there, boated there, and simply soaked in the beauty of being there.

We've gone up Mount Washington, both in car and on motorcycle. And we saw the Old Man in the Mountain numerous times before it rejoined nature.

Robert Frost was born in 1874 in San Francisco. His father died in 1885, when he was only 11, and the family moved to Massachusetts to be with the grandfather.

Frost first published *New Hampshire* in 1923, and it won the Pulitzer Prize. No wonder. With gems like "Stopping by Woods on a Snowy Evening" and "Nothing Gold Can Stay", it's a true treasure-house. These are the sorts of poems I love quoting while we go walking in the woods.

I'm an enormous fan of Frost. He is incredibly inspiring. He really brings what is precious about New Hampshire to life. I hope you enjoy these poems as much as I do.

I'd love to hear your thoughts!

The proceeds from this book support local arts programs.

New Hampshire

I met a lady from the South who said
(You won't believe she said it, but she said it):
"None of my family ever worked, or had
A thing to sell." I don't suppose the work
Much matters. You may work for all of me.
I've seen the time I've had to work myself.
The having anything to sell is what
Is the disgrace in man or state or nation.

I met a traveler from Arkansas
Who boasted of his state as beautiful
For diamonds and apples. "Diamonds
And apples in commercial quantities?"
I asked him, on my guard. "Oh, yes," he answered,
Off his. The time was evening in the Pullman.
"I see the porter's made your bed," I told him.

I met a Californian who would
Talk California—a state so blessed,
He said, in climate, none bad ever died there
A natural death, and Vigilance Committees
Had had to organize to stock the graveyards
And vindicate the state's humanity.
"Just the way Stefansson runs on," I murmured,
"About the British Arctic. That's what comes
Of being in the market with a climate."

I met a poet from another state,
A zealot full of fluid inspiration,
Who in the name of fluid inspiration,
But in the best style of bad salesmanship,
Angrily tried to make me write a protest
(In verse I think) against the Volstead Act.
He didn't even offer me a drink
Until I asked for one to steady him.
This is called having an idea to sell.

It never could have happened in New Hampshire.

The only person really soiled with trade
I ever stumbled on in old New Hampshire
Was someone who had just come back ashamed
From selling things in California.
He'd built a noble mansard roof with balls
On turrets, like Constantinople, deep
In woods some ten miles from a railroad station,
As if to put forever out of mind
The hope of being, as we say, received.
I found him standing at the close of day
Inside the threshold of his open barn,
Like a lone actor on a gloomy stage—
And recognized him, through the iron gray
In which his face was muffled to the eyes,
As an old boyhood friend, and once indeed
A drover with me on the road to Brighton.
His farm was "grounds," and not a farm at all;

His house among the local sheds and shanties
Rose like a factor's at a trading station.
And be was rich, and I was still a rascal.
I couldn't keep from asking impolitely,
Where bad he been and what had he been doing?
How did he get so? (Rich was understood.)
In dealing in "old rags" in San Francisco.
Ob, it was terrible as well could be.
We both of us turned over in our graves.

Just specimens is all New Hampshire has,
One each of everything as in a showcase,
Which naturally she doesn't care to sell.

She had one President. (Pronounce him Purse,
And make the most of it for better or worse.
He's your one chance to score against the state.)
She had one Daniel Webster. He was all
The Daniel Webster ever was or shall be.
She had the Dartmouth' needed to produce him.

I call her old. She has one family
Whose claim is good to being settled here
Before the era of colonization,
And before that of exploration even.
John Smith remarked them as be coasted by,
Dangling their legs and fishing off a wharf
At the Isles of Shoals, and satisfied himself
They weren't Red Indians but veritable
Pre-primitives of the white race, dawn people,

Like those who furnished Adam's sons with wives;
However uninnocent they may have been
In being there so early in our history.
They'd been there then a hundred years or more.
Pity he didn't ask what they were up to
At that date with a wharf already built,
And take their name. They've since told me their name—
Today an honored one in Nottingham.
As for what they were up to more than fishing—
Suppose they weren't behaving Puritanly,
The hour bad not yet struck for being good,
Mankind had not yet gone on the Sabbatical.
It became an explorer of the deep
Not to explore too deep in others' business.

Did you but know of him, New Hampshire has
One real reformer who would change the world
So it would be accepted by two classes,
Artists the minute they set up as artists,
Before, that is, they are themselves accepted,
And boys the minute they get out of college.
I can't help thinking those are tests to go by.

And she has one I don't know what to call him,
Who comes from Philadelphia every year
With a great flock of chickens of rare breeds
He wants to give the educational
Advantages of growing almost wild
Under the watchful eye of hawk and eagle
Dorkings because they're spoken of by Chaucer,

Sussex because they're spoken of by Herrick.

She has a touch of gold. New Hampshire gold—
You may have heard of it. I had a farm
Offered me not long since up Berlin way
With a mine on it that was worked for gold;
But not gold in commercial quantities,
Just enough gold to make the engagement rings
And marriage rings of those who owned the farm.
What gold more innocent could one have asked for?
One of my children ranging after rocks
Lately brought home from Andover or Canaan
A specimen of beryl with a trace
Of radium. I know with radium
The trace would have to be the merest trace
To be below the threshold of commercial;
But trust New Hampshire not to have enough
Of radium or anything to sell.

A specimen of everything, I said.
She has one witch—old style. She lives in Colebrook.
(The only other witch I ever met
Was lately at a cut-glass dinner in Boston.
There were four candles and four people present.
The witch was young, and beautiful (new style),
And open-minded. She was free to question
Her gift for reading letters locked in boxes.
Why was it so much greater when the boxes
Were metal than it was when they were wooden?
It made the world seem so mysterious.

The S'ciety for Psychical Research
Was cognizant. Her husband was worth millions.
I think he owned some shares in Harvard College.)

New Hampshire used to have at Salem
A company we called the White Corpuscles,
Whose duty was at any hour of night
To rush in sheets and fool's caps where they smelled
A thing the least bit doubtfully presented
And give someone the Skipper Ireson's Ride.

One each of everything as in a showcase.

More than enough land for a specimen
You'll say she has, but there there enters in
Something else to protect her from herself.
There quality makes up for quantity.
Not even New Hampshire farms are much for sale.
The farm I made my home on in the mountains
1 had to take by force rather than buy.

I caught the owner outdoors by himself
Raking.up after winter, and I said,
"I'm going to put you off this farm: I want it."
"Where are you going to put me? In the road?"
"I'm going to put you on the farm next to it."
"Why won't the farm next to it do for you?"
"I like this better." It was really better.

Apples? New Hampshire has them, but unsprayed,

With no suspicion in stern end or blossom end
Of vitriol or arsenate of lead,
And so not good for anything but cider.
Her unpruned grapes are flung like lariats
Far up the birches out of reach of man.

A state producing precious metals, stones,
And—writing; none of these except perhaps
The precious literature in quantity
Or quality to worry the producer
About disposing of it. Do you know,
Considering the market, there are more
Poems produced than any other thing?
No wonder poets sometimes have to seem
So much more businesslike than businessmen.
Their wares are so much harder to get rid of.

She's one of the two best states in the Union.
Vermont's the other. And the two have been
Yokefellows in the sap yoke from of old
In many Marches. And they lie like wedges,
Thick end to thin end and thin end to thick end,
And are a figure of the way the strong
Of mind and strong of arm should fit together,
One thick where one is thin and vice versa.

New Hampshire raises the Connecticut

In a trout hatchery near Canada,
But soon divides the river with Vermont.

Both are delightful states for their absurdly
Small towns—Lost Nation, Bungey, Muddy Boo,
Poplin, Still Corners (so called not because
The place is silent all day long, nor yet
Because it boasts a whisky still—because
It set out once to be a city and still
Is only corners, crossroads in a wood).
And I remember one whose name appeared
Between the pictures on a movie screen
Election night once in Franconia,
When everything had gone Republican
And Democrats were sore in need of comfort:
Easton goes Democratic, Wilson 4
Hughes 2. And everybody to the saddest
Laughed the loud laugh the big laugh at the little.
New York (five million) laughs at Manchester,
Manchester (sixty or seventy thousand) laughs
At Littleton (four thousand), Littleton
Laughs at Franconia (seven hundred), and
Franconia laughs, I fear—-did laugh that night---
At Easton. What has Easton left to laugh at,
And like the actress exclaim "Oh, my God" at?
There's Bungey; and for Bungey there are towns,
Whole townships named but without population.

Anything I can say about New Hampshire
Will serve almost as well about Vermont,
Excepting that they differ in their mountains.
The Vermont mountains stretch extended straight;
New Hampshire mountains Curl up in a coil.

I had been coming to New Hampshire mountains.
And here I am and what am I to say?
Here first my theme becomes embarrassing.
Emerson said, "The God who made New Hampshire
Taunted the lofty land with little men."
Another Massachusetts poet said,
"I go no more to summer in New Hampshire.
I've given up my summer place in Dublin."
But when I asked to know what ailed New Hampshire,
She said she couldn't stand the people in it,
The little men (it's Massachusetts speaking).
And when I asked to know what ailed the people,
She said, "Go read your own books and find out."
I may as well confess myself the author
Of several books against the world in general.
To take them as against a special state
Or even nation's to restrict my meaning.
I'm what is called a sensibilitist,
Or otherwise an environmentalist.
I refuse to adapt myself a mite
To any change from hot to cold, from wet
To dry, from poor to rich, or back again.
I make a virtue of my suffering
From nearly everything that goes on round me.
In other words, I know wherever I am,
Being the creature of literature I am,
I shall not lack for pain to keep me awake.
Kit Marlowe taught me how to say my prayers:
"Why, this is Hell, nor am I out of it."

Samoa, Russia, Ireland I complain of,
No less than England, France, and Italy.
Because I wrote my novels in New Hampshire
Is no proof that I aimed them at New Hampshire.
When I left Massachusetts years ago
Between two days, the reason why I sought
New Hampshire, not Connecticut,
Rhode Island, New York, or Vermont was this:
Where I was living then, New Hampshire offered
The nearest boundary to escape across.
I hadn't an illusion in my handbag
About the people being better there
Than those I left behind. I thought they weren't.
I thought they couldn't be. And yet they were.
I'd sure had no such friends in Massachusetts
As Hall of Windham, Gay of Atkinson,
Bartlett of Raymond (now of Colorado),
Harris of Derry, and Lynch of Bethlehem.

The glorious bards of Massachusetts seem
To want to make New Hampshire people over.
They taunt the lofty land with little men.
I don't know what to say about the people.
For art's sake one could almost wish them worse
Rather than better. How are we to write
The Russian novel in America
As long as life goes so unterribly?
There is the pinch from which our only outcry
In literature to date is heard to come.
We get what little misery we can

Out of not having cause for misery.
It makes the guild of novel writers sick
To be expected to be Dostoievskis
On nothing worse than too much luck and comfort.
This is not sorrow, though; it's just the vapors,
And recognized as such in Russia itself
Under the new regime, and so forbidden.

If well it is with Russia, then feel free
To say so or be stood against the wall
And shot. It's Pollyanna now or death.
This, then, is the new freedom we hear tell of;
And very sensible. No state can build
A literature that shall at once be sound
And sad on a foundation of well-being.

To show the level of intelligence
Among us: it was just a Warren farmer
Whose horse had pulled him short up in the road
By me, a stranger. This is what he said,
From nothing but embarrassment and want
Of anything more sociable to say:
"You hear those bound dogs sing on Moosilauke?
Well, they remind me of the hue and cry
We've heard against the Mid - Victorians
And never rightly understood till Bryan
Retired from politics and joined the chorus.
The matter with the Mid-Victorians
Seems to have been a man named Joh n L. Darwin."
"Go 'long," I said to him, he to his horse.

I knew a man who failing as a farmer
Burned down his farmhouse for the fire insurance,
And spent the proceeds on a telescope
To satisfy a lifelong curiosity
About our place among the infinities.
And how was that for otherworldliness?

If I must choose which I would elevate —
The people or the already lofty mountains
I'd elevate the already lofty mountains
The only fault I find with old New Hampshire
Is that her mountains aren't quite high enough.
I was not always so; I've come to be so.
How, to my sorrow, how have I attained
A height from which to look down critical
On mountains? What has given me assurance
To say what height becomes New Hampshire mountains,
Or any mountains? Can it be some strength
I feel, as of an earthquake in my back,
To heave them higher to the morning star?
Can it be foreign travel in the Alps?
Or having seen and credited a moment
The solid molding of vast peaks of cloud
Behind the pitiful reality
Of Lincoln, Lafayette, and Liberty?
Or some such sense as says bow high shall jet
The fountain in proportion to the basin?
No, none of these has raised me to my throne
Of intellectual dissatisfaction,

But the sad accident of having seen
Our actual mountains given in a map
Of early times as twice the height they are—
Ten thousand feet instead of only five—
Which shows how sad an accident may be.
Five thousand is no longer high enough.
Whereas I never had a good idea
About improving people in the world,
Here I am overfertile in suggestion,
And cannot rest from planning day or night
How high I'd thrust the peaks in summer snow
To tap the upper sky and draw a flow
Of frosty night air on the vale below
Down from the stars to freeze the dew as starry.

The more the sensibilitist I am
The more I seem to want my mountains wild;
The way the wiry gang-boss liked the logjam.
After he'd picked the lock and got it started,
He dodged a log that lifted like an arm
Against the sky to break his back for him,
Then came in dancing, skipping with his life
Across the roar and chaos, and the words
We saw him say along the zigzag journey
Were doubtless as the words we heard him say
On coming nearer: "Wasn't she an i-deal
Son-of-a-bitch? You bet she was an i-deal."

For all her mountains fall a little short,
Her people not quite short enough for Art,

She's still New Hampshire; a most restful state.

Lately in converse with a New York alec
About the new school of the pseudo-phallic,
I found myself in a close corner where
I bad to make an almost funny choice.
"Choose you which you will be—a prude, or puke,
Mewling and puking in the public arms."
"Me for the hills where I don't have to choose."
"But if you bad to choose, which would you be?"
1 wouldn't be a prude afraid of nature.
I know a man who took a double ax
And went alone against a grove of trees;
But his heart failing him, he dropped the ax
And ran for shelter quoting Matthew Arnold:
"'Nature is cruel, man is sick of blood':
There's been enough shed without shedding mine.
Remember Birnam Wood! The wood's in flux!"

He had a special terror of the flux
That showed itself in dendrophobia.
The only decent tree had been to mill
And educated into boards, be said.
He knew too well for any earthly use
The line where man leaves off and nature starts.
And never overstepped it save in dreams.
He stood on the safe side of the line talking—
Which is sheer Matthew Arnoldism,
The cult of one who owned himself "a foiled
Circuitous wanderer," and "took dejectedly

His seat upon the intellectual throne"—
Agreed in 'frowning on these improvised
Altars the woods are full of nowadays,
Again as in the days when Ahaz sinned
By worship under green trees in the open.
Scarcely a mile but that I come on one,
A black-checked stone and stick of rain-washed charcoal.
Even to say the groves were God's first temples
Comes too near to Ahaz' sin for safety.
Nothing not built with hands of course is sacred.
But here is not a question of what's sacred;
Rather of what to face or run away from.
I'd hate to be a runaway from nature.
And neither would I choose to be a puke
Who cares not what he does in company,
And when he can't do anything, falls back
On words, and tries his worst to make words speak
Louder than actions, and sometimes achieves it.
It seems a narrow choice the age insists on
8ow about being a good Greek, for instance)
That course, they tell me, isn't offered this year.
"Come, but this isn't choosing—puke or prude?"

Well, if I have to choose one or the other,
I choose to be a plain New Hampshire farmer
With an income in cash of, say, a thousand
(From, say, a publisher in New York City).
It's restful to arrive at a decision,
And restful just to think about New Hampshire.
At present I am living in Vermont.

NOTES

Wow, talk about a mouthful to start out this series! And it's not even a neatly rhymed poem like the classic Woods. It's more freeform, more flowing, like hanging out on the porch bench at a general store during a motorcycle ride and hearing a local friend tell you how things are going.

And I think that's the beauty of this. It draws you in. You have a cup of tea, or a glass of wine, and you soak into the atmosphere.

It's the perfect introduction to New Hampshire.

A Star in a Stone-Boat

For Lincoln MacVeagh

Never tell me that not one star of all
That slip from heaven at night and softly fall
Has been picked up with stones to build a wall.

Some laborer found one faded and stone-cold,
And saving that its weight suggested gold
And tugged it from his first too certain hold,

He noticed nothing in it to remark.
He was not used to handling stars thrown dark
And lifeless from an interrupted arc.

He did not recognize in that smooth coal
The one thing palpable besides the soul
To penetrate the air in which we roll.

He did not see how like a flying thing
It brooded ant eggs, and bad one large wing,
One not so large for flying in a ring,

And a long Bird of Paradise's tail
(Though these when not in use to fly and trail
It drew back in its body like a snail);

Nor know that he might move it from the spot—
The harm was done: from having been star-shot
The very nature of the soil was hot

And burning to yield flowers instead of grain,
Flowers fanned and not put out by all the rain
Poured on them by his prayers prayed in vain.

He moved it roughly with an iron bar,
He loaded an old stoneboat with the star
And not, as you might think, a flying car,

Such as even poets would admit perforce
More practical than Pegasus the horse
If it could put a star back in its course.

He dragged it through the plowed ground at a pace
But faintly reminiscent of the race
Of jostling rock in interstellar space.

It went for building stone, and I, as though
Commanded in a dream, forever go
To right the wrong that this should have been so.

Yet ask where else it could have gone as well,
I do not know—I cannot stop to tell:
He might have left it lying where it fell.

From following walls I never lift my eye,
Except at night to places in the sky

Where showers of charted meteors let fly.

Some may know what they seek in school and church,
And why they seek it there; for what I search
I must go measuring stone walls, perch on perch;

Sure that though not a star of death and birth,
So not to be compared, perhaps, in worth
To such resorts of life as Mars and Earth—

Though not, I say, a star of death and sin,
It yet has poles, and only needs a spin
To show its worldly nature and begin

To chafe and shuffle in my calloused palm
And run off in strange tangents with my arm,
As fish do with the line in first alarm.

Such as it is, it promises the prize
Of the one world complete in any size
That I am like to compass, fool or wise.

NOTES

This one is definitely much more manageable, now that we're actually "into" the poetry set. It creates fun images and, for those of us who live around here, we have stone walls everywhere. The idea of a fallen star becoming part of a stone wall makes perfect sense.

My father loves genealogy and local history. On weekends when I was young we used to go out hiking in forests in Connecticut looking for ancient foundations and stone walls. My current house in Massachusetts has stone walls on the three sides of it. It feels very cozy. This is the back yard.

The Census-Taker

I came an errand one cloud-blowing evening
To a slab-built, black-paper-covered house
Of one room and one window and one door,
The only dwelling in a waste cut over
A hundred square miles round it in the mountains:
And that not dwelt in now by men or women.
(It never had been dwelt in, though, by women,
So what is this I make a sorrow of?)
I came as census-taker to the waste
To count the people in it and found none,
None in the hundred miles, none in the house,
Where I came last with some hope, but not much,
After hours' overlooking from the cliffs
An emptiness flayed to the very stone.
I found no people that dared show themselves,
None not in hiding from the outward eye.
The time was autumn, but how anyone
could tell the time of year when every tree
That could have dropped a leaf was down itself
And nothing but the stump of it was left
Now bringing out its rings in sugar of pitch;
And every tree up stood a rotting trunk
Without a single leaf to spend on autumn,
Or branch to whistle after what was spent.
Perhaps the wind the more without the help
Of breathing trees said something of the time

Of year or day the way it swung a door
Forever off the latch, as if rude men
Passed in and slammed it shut each one behind him
For the next one to open for himself.
I counted nine I had no right to count
(But this was dreamy unofficial counting)
Before I made the tenth across the threshold.
Where was my supper? Where was anyone's?
No lamp was lit. Nothing was on the table.
The stove was cold—the stove was off the chimney—
And down by one side where it lacked a leg.
The people that had loudly passed the door
Were people to the ear but not the eye.
They were not on the table with their elbows.
They were not sleeping in the shelves of bunks.
I saw no men there and no bones of men there.
I armed myself against such bones as might be
With the pitch-blackened stub of an ax-handle
I picked up off the straw-dust-covered floor.
Not bones, but the ill-fitted window rattled.
The door was still because I held it shut
While I thought what to do that could be done—
About the house—about the people not there.
This house in one year fallen to decay
Filled me with no less sorrow than the houses
Fallen to ruin in ten thousand years
Where Asia wedges Africa from Europe.
Nothing was left to do that I could see
Unless to find that there was no one there
And declare to the cliffs too far for echo,

"The place is desert, and let whoso lurks
In silence, if in this he is aggrieved,
Break silence now or be forever silent.
Let him say why it should not be declared so."
The melancholy of having to count souls
Where they grow fewer and fewer every year
Is extreme where they shrink to none at all.
It must be I want life to go on living.

NOTES

I love this poem. I do a lot of genealogy, as does my father and as did my grandmother. We deal with census records quite a lot. My boyfriend did the local census during the last pass and it was a fascinating process.

I can definitely feel the sad loneliness of someone wanting to count locals, to keep the local culture alive, but they're just not there any more. They're fading away. It's being lost and there's no way to stop it.

We can think of landscapes as quaint, but fewer people want to live in places like that. Places with no fast internet. Places far from stores and restaurants. Places where it's easy to get snowbound for days.

The Star-Splitter

"You know Orion always comes up sideways.
Throwing a leg up over our fence of mountains,
And rising on his hands, he looks in on me
Busy outdoors by lantern-light with something
I should have done by daylight, and indeed,
After the ground is frozen, I should have done
Before it froze, and a gust flings a handful
Of waste leaves at my smoky lantern chimney
To make fun of my way of doing things,
Or else fun of Orion's having caught me.
Has a man, I should like to ask, no rights
These forces are obliged to pay respect to?"
So Brad McLaughlin mingled reckless talk
Of heavenly stars with hugger-mugger farming,
Till having failed at hugger-mugger farming
He burned his house down for the fire insurance
And spent the proceeds on a telescope
To satisfy a lifelong curiosity
About our place among the infinities.

"What do you want with one of those blame things?"
I asked him well beforehand. "Don't you get one!"

"Don't call it blamed; there isn't anything
More blameless in the sense of being less
A weapon in our human fight," he said.

"I'll have one if I sell my farm to buy it."
There where he moved the rocks to plow the ground
And plowed between the rocks he couldn't move,
Few farms changed hands; so rather than spend years
Trying to sell his farm and then not selling,
He burned his house down for the fire insurance
And bought the telescope with what it came to.
He had been heard to say by several:
"The best thing that we're put here for's to see;
The strongest thing that's given us to see with's
A telescope. Someone in every town
Seems to me owes it to the town to keep one.
In Littleton it might as well be me."
After such loose talk it was no surprise
When he did what he did and burned his house down.

Mean laughter went about the town that day
To let him know we weren't the least imposed on,
And he could wait---we'd see to him tomorrow.
But the first thing next morning we reflected
If one by one we counted people out
For the least sin, it wouldn't take us long
To get so we had no one left to live with.
For to be social is to be forgiving.
Our thief, the one who does our stealing from us,
We don't cut off from coming to church suppers,
But what we miss we go to him and ask for.
He promptly gives it back, that is if still
Uneaten, unworn out, or undisposed of.
It wouldn't do to be too hard on Brad

About his telescope. Beyond the age
Of being given one for Christmas gift,
He had to take the best way he knew how
To find himself in one. Well, all we said was
He took a strange thing to be roguish over.
Some sympathy was wasted on the house,
A good old-timer dating back along;
But a house isn't sentient; the house
Didn't feel anything. And if it did,
Why not regard it as a sacrifice,
And an old-fashioned sacrifice by fire,
Instead of a new-fashioned one at auction?

Out of a house and so out of a farm
At one stroke (of a match), Brad had to turn
To earn a living on the Concord railroad,
As under-ticket-agent at a station
Where his job, when he wasn't selling tickets,
Was setting out, up track and down, not plants
As on a farm, but planets, evening stars
That varied in their hue from red to green.

He got a good glass for six hundred dollars.
His new job gave him leisure for stargazing.
Often he bid me come and have a look
Up the brass barrel, velvet black inside,
At a star quaking in the other end.
I recollect a night of broken clouds
And underfoot snow melted down to ice,
And melting further in the wind to mud.

Bradford and I had out the telescope.
We spread our two legs as we spread its three,
Pointed our thoughts the way we pointed it,
And standing at our leisure till the day broke,
Said some of the best things we ever said.
That telescope was christened the Star-Splitter,
Because it didn't do a thing but split
A star in two or three, the way you split
A globule of quicksilver in your hand
With one stroke of your finger in the middle.
It's a star-splitter if there ever was one,
And ought to do some good if splitting stars
'Sa thing to be compared with splitting wood.

We've looked and looked, but after all where are we?
Do we know any better where we are,
And how it stands between the night tonight
And a man with a smoky lantern chimney?
How different from the way it ever stood?

NOTES

Another poem I really adore. We had a telescope for many years and would have lots of fun searching out stars, planets, and carefully viewing eclipses. We'd do things like redirect it onto random household objects. This was done in the snow.

There was also a person who hung out on a web forum I used who used to say her parents were frustrated with the house and wished it would just burn down. A few months later, sure enough, it did. So these things do happen. Frustration builds and then something just snaps.

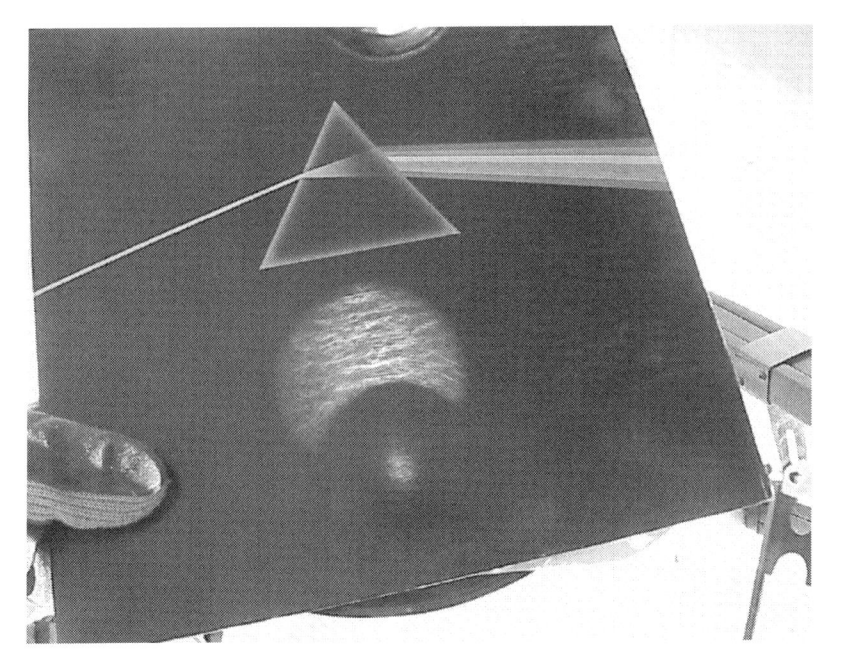

Maple

Her teacher's certainty it must be Mabel
Made Maple first take notice of her name.
She asked her father and he told her, "Maple—
Maple is right."
"But teacher told the school
There's no such name."
"Teachers don't know as much
As fathers about children, you tell teacher.
You tell her that it's M-A-P-L-E.
You ask her if she knows a maple tree.
Well, you were named after a maple tree.
Your mother named you. You and she just saw
Each other in passing in the room upstairs,
One coming this way into life, and one
Going the other out of life—you know?
So you can't have much recollection of her.
She had been having a long look at you.
She put her finger in your cheek so hard
It must have made your dimple there, and said,
'Maple.' I said it too: 'Yes, for her name.'
She nodded. So we're sure there's no mistake.
I don't know what she wanted it to mean,
But it seems like some word she left to bid you
Be a good girl—be like a maple tree.
How like a maple tree's for us to guess.
Or for a little girl to guess sometime.

Not now—at least I shouldn't try too hard now.
By and by I will tell you all I know
About the different trees, and something, too,
About your mother that perhaps may help."
Dangerous self-arousing words to sow.
Luckily all she wanted of her name then
Was to rebuke her teacher with it next day,
And give the teacher a scare as from her father.
Anything further had been wasted on her,
Or so he tried to think to avoid blame.
She would forget it. She all but forgot it.
What he sowed with her slept so long a sleep,
And came so near death in the dark of years,
That when it woke and came to life again
The flower was different from the parent seed.
It carne back vaguely at the glass one day,
As she stood saying her name over aloud,
Striking it gently across her lowered eyes
To make it go well with the way she looked.
What was it about her name? Its strangeness lay
In having too much meaning. Other names,
As Lesley, Carol, Irma, Marjorie,
Signified nothing. Rose could have a meaning,
But hadn't as it went. (She knew a Rose.)
This difference from other names it was
Made people notice it—and notice her.
(They either noticed it, or got it wrong.)
Her problem was to find out what it asked
In dress or manner of the girl who bore it.
If she could form some notion of her mother—

What she bad thought was lovely, and what good.
This was her mother's childhood home;
The house one story high in front, three stories
On the end it presented to the road.
(The arrangement made a pleasant sunny cellar.)
Her mother's bedroom was her father's still,
Where she could watch her mother's picture fading.
Once she found for a bookmark in the Bible
A maple leaf she thought must have been laid
In wait for her there. She read every word
Of the two pages it was pressed between,
As if it was her mother speaking to her.
But forgot to put the leaf back in closing
And lost the place never to read again.
She was sure, though, there had been nothing in it.

So she looked for herself, as everyone
Looks for himself, more or less outwardly.
And her self-seeking, fitful though it was,
May still have been what led her on to read,
And think a little, and get some city schooling.
She learned shorthand, whatever shorthand may
Have had to do with it--she sometimes wondered.
So, till she found herself in a strange place
For the name Maple to have brought her to,
Taking dictation on a paper pad
And, in the pauses when she raised her eyes,
Watching out of a nineteenth story window
An airship laboring with unshiplike motion
And a vague all-disturbing roar above the river

Beyond the highest city built with hands.
Someone was saying in such natural tones
She almost wrote the words down on her knee,
"Do you know you remind me of a tree--
A maple tree?"

"Because my name is Maple?"
"Isn't it Mabel? I thought it was Mabel."

"No doubt you've heard the office call me Mabel.
I have to let them call me what they like."

They were both stirred that he should have divined
Without the name her personal mystery.
It made it seem as if there must be something
She must have missed herself. So they were married,
And took the fancy home with them to live by.

They went on pilgrimage once to her father's
(The house one story high in front, three stories
On the side it presented to the road)
To see if there was not some special tree
She might have overlooked. They could find none,
Not so much as a single tree for shade,
Let alone grove of trees for sugar orchard.
She told him of the bookmark maple leaf
In the big Bible, and all she remembered
of the place marked with it—"Wave offering,
Something about wave offering, it said."

"You've never asked your father outright, have you?"

"I have, and been put off sometime, I think."
(This was her faded memory of the way
Once long ago her father had put himself off.)
"Because no telling but it may have been
Something between your father and your mother
Not meant for us at all."
"Not meant for me?
Where would the fairness be in giving me
A name to carry for life and never know
The secret of?"
"And then it may have been
Something a father couldn't tell a daughter
As well as could a mother. And again
It may have been their one lapse into fancy
'Twould be too bad to make him sorry for
By bringing it up to him when be was too old.
Your father feels us round him with our questing,
And holds us off unnecessarily,
As if he didn't know what little thing
Might lead us on to a discovery.
It was as personal as be could be
About the way he saw it was with you
To say your mother, bad she lived, would be
As far again as from being born to bearing."

"Just one look more with what you say in mind,
And I give up"; which last look came to nothing.
But though they now gave up the search forever,

They clung to what one had seen in the other
By inspiration. It proved there was something.
They kept their thoughts away from when the maples
Stood uniform in buckets, and the steam
Of sap and snow rolled off the sugarhouse.
When they made her related to the maples,
It was the tree the autumn fire ran through
And swept of leathern leaves, but left the bark
Unscorched, unblackened, even, by any smoke.
They always took their holidays in autumn.
Once they came on a maple in a glade,
Standing alone with smooth arms lifted up,
And every leaf of foliage she'd worn
Laid scarlet and pale pink about her feet.
But its age kept them from considering this one.
Twenty-five years ago at Maple's naming
It hardly could have been a two-leaved seedling
The next cow might have licked up out at pasture.
Could it have been another maple like it?
They hovered for a moment near discovery,
Figurative enough to see the symbol,
But lacking faith in anything to mean
The same at different times to different people.
Perhaps a filial diffidence partly kept them
From thinking it could be a thing so bridal.
And anyway it came too late for Maple.
She used her hands to cover up her eyes.

"We would not see the secret if we could now:
We are not looking for it any more."

Thus had a name with meaning, given in death,
Made a girl's marriage, and ruled in her life.
No matter that the meaning was not clear.
A name with meaning could bring up a child,
Taking the child out of the parents' hands.
Better a meaningless name, I should say,
As leaving more to nature and happy chance.
Name children some names and see what you do.

NOTES

I love this one. The story sucks you in. You want to know what the name means and you never find out – but it impacted her anyway. It wove its way into her life. And the imagery is, of course, lovely.

I love all seasons here in New England but autumn is absolutely the best. I adore the foliage. It is just beautiful. Here's a foliage photo from New Hampshire. And most of the colors come from the maple trees. It's from *Someone35*.

If I was named maple I think I'd dress in its colors for each season. Fall would be delightful.

The Ax-Helve

I've known ere now an interfering branch
Of alder catch my lifted ax behind me.
But that was in the woods, to hold my hand
From striking at another alder's roots,
And that was, as I say, an alder branch.
This was a man, Baptiste, who stole one day
Behind me on the snow in my own yard
Where I was working at the chopping block,
And cutting nothing not cut down already.
He caught my ax expertly on the rise,
When all my strength put forth was in his favor,
Held it a moment where it was, to calm me,
Then took it from me — and I let him take it.
I didn't know him well enough to know
What it was all about. There might be something
He had in mind to say to a bad neighbor
He might prefer to say to him disarmed.
But all he had to tell me in French-English
Was what he thought of— not me, but my ax;
Me only as I took my ax to heart.
It was the bad ax-helve some one had sold me —
"Made on machine," he said, plowing the grain
With a thick thumbnail to show how it ran
Across the handle's long-drawn serpentine,
Like the two strokes across a dollar sign.
"You give her 'one good crack, she's snap raght off.

Den where's your hax-ead flying t'rough de hair?"
Admitted; and yet, what was that to him?

"Come on my house and I put you one in
What's las' awhile — good hick'ry what's grow crooked,
De second growt' I cut myself—tough, tough!"

Something to sell? That wasn't how it sounded.

"Den when you say you come? It's cost you nothing.
To-naght?"

As well to-night as any night.

Beyond an over-warmth of kitchen stove
My welcome differed from no other welcome.
Baptiste knew best why I was where I was.
So long as he would leave enough unsaid,
I shouldn't mind his being overjoyed
(If overjoyed he was) at having got me
Where I must judge if what he knew about an ax
That not everybody else knew was to count
For nothing in the measure of a neighbor.
Hard if, though cast away for life with Yankees,
A Frenchman couldn't get his human rating!

Mrs. Baptiste came in and rocked a chair
That had as many motions as the world:
One back and forward, in and out of shadow,
That got her nowhere; one more gradual,

Sideways, that would have run her on the stove
In time, had she not realized her danger
And caught herself up bodily, chair and all,
And set herself back where she started from.
"She ain't spick too much Henglish— dat's too bad."
I was afraid, in brightening first on me,
Then on Baptiste, as if she understood
What passed between us, she was only reigning.
Baptiste was anxious for her; but no more
Than for himself, so placed he couldn't hope
To keep his bargain of the morning with me
In time to keep me from suspecting him
Of really never having meant to keep it.

Needlessly soon he had his ax-helves out,
A quiverful to choose from, since he wished me
To have the best he had, or had to spare —
Not for me to ask which, when what he took
Had beauties he had to point me out at length
To ensure their not being wasted on me.
He liked to have it slender as a whipstock,
Free from the least knot, equal to the strain
Of bending like a sword across the knee.
He showed me that the lines of a good helve
Were native to the grain before the knife
Expressed them, and its curves were no false curves
Put on it from without. And there its strength lay
For the hard work. He chafed its long white body
From end to end with his rough hand shut round it.
He tried it at the eye-hold in the ax-head.

"Hahn, hahn," he mused, "don't need much taking down."
Baptiste knew how to make a short job long
For love of it, and yet not waste time either.

Do you know, what we talked about was knowledge?
Baptiste on his defense about the children
He kept from school, or did his best to keep —
Whatever school and children and our doubts
Of laid-on education had to do
With the curves of his ax-helves and his having
Used these unscrupulously to bring me
To see for once the inside of his house.
Was I desired in friendship, partly as someone
To leave it to, whether the right to hold
Such doubts of education should depend
Upon the education of those who held them.

But now he brushed the shavings from his knee
And stood the ax there on its horse's hoof,
Erect, but not without its waves, as when
The snake stood up for evil in the Garden—
Top-heavy with a heaviness his short,
Thick hand made light of, steel-blue chin drawn down
And in a little — a French touch in that.
Baptiste drew back and squinted at it, pleased:
"See how she's cock her head!"

NOTES

Another one that I just love. I can see the scenes, feel the crisp snow, feel the catch in the ax swing. And I can get the sense of the couple, not handling English well, wanting to make a connection. It's full of great details that really settle me into the scene.

You have to love snow, living here in New England. I absolutely adore it. To be fair, Bob does all the shoveling. I work from home. So I get to love it falling and then love it being prettily all around the house. And then he goes out and makes paths in the snow.

If we get a good snow of a foot or more I'll put on my high boots and go tromping in the back yard to make a meditation spiral. I'll work my way around, in, in, to its center. And then I'll walk out again. I always hope it will someday show up on Google's satellite maps.

Luke MacNeil

The Grindstone

Having a wheel and four legs of its own
Has never availed the cumbersome grindstone
To get it anywhere that I can see.
These hands have helped it go, and even race;
Not all the motion, though, they ever lent,
Not all the miles it may have thought it went,
Have got it one step from the starting place.
It stands beside the same old apple tree.
The shadow of the apple tree is thin
Upon it now its feet as fast in snow.
All other farm machinery's gone in,
And some of it on no more legs and wheel
Than the grindstone can boast to stand or go.
(I'm thinking chiefly of the wheelbarrow.)
For months it hasn't known the taste of steel
Washed down with rusty water in a tin.
But standing outdoors hungry, in the cold,
Except in towns at night is not a sin.
And, anyway, it's standing in the yard
Under a ruinous live apple tree
Has nothing any more to do with me,
Except that I remember how of old
One summer day, all day I drove it hard,
And someone mounted on it rode it hard
And he and I between us ground a blade.
I gave it the preliminary spin

And poured on water (tears it might have been);
And when it almost gaily jumped and flowed,
A Father-Time-like man got on and rode,
Armed with a scythe and spectacles that glowed.
He turned on will-power to increase the load
And slow me down -- and I abruptly slowed,
Like coming to a sudden railroad station.
I changed from hand to hand in desperation.
I wondered what machine of ages gone
This represented an improvement on.
For all I knew it may have sharpened spears
And arrowheads itself. Much use for years
Had gradually worn it an oblate
Spheroid that kicked and struggled in its gait,
Appearing to return me hate for hate;
(But I forgive it now as easily
As any other boyhood enemy
Whose pride has failed to get him anywhere).
I wondered who it was the man thought ground
-The one who held the wheel back or the one
Who gave his life to keep it going round?
I wondered if he really thought it fair
For him to have the say when we were done.
Such were the bitter thoughts to which I turned.
Not for myself was I so much concerned
Oh no --Although, of course, I could have found
A better way to pass the afternoon
Than grinding discord out of a grindstone,
And beating insects at their gritty tune.
Nor was I for the man so much concerned.

Once when the grindstone almost jumped its bearing
It looked as if he might be badly thrown
And wounded on his blade. So far from caring,
I laughed inside, and only cranked the faster
(It ran as if it wasn't greased but glued);
I'd welcome any moderate disaster
That might be calculated to postpone
What evidently nothing could conclude.
The thing that made me more and more afraid
Was that we'd ground it sharp and hadn't known,
And now were only wasting precious blade.
And when he raised it dripping once and tried
The creepy edge of it with wary touch
And viewed it over his glasses funny-eyed,
Only disinterestedly to decide
It needed a turn more, I could have cried
Wasn't there a danger of a turn too much?
Mightn't we make it worse instead of better?
I was for leaving something to the wetter.
What if it wasn't all it should be? I'd
Be satisfied if he'd be satisfied.

NOTES

Frost is just so amazing with his scenes and details. I admit I've never owned a grindstone. However, I'm only a half hour from Old Sturbridge Village which is an 1840s historic town with all sorts of great authentic buildings. This isn't one of the grindstones, but it's the sawmill which is just amazing when it's in motion.

In any case, having seen these things in action, I can really see the scenes he describes.

Paul's Wife

To drive Paul out of any lumber camp
All that was needed was to say to him,
"How is the wife, Paul?"--and he'd disappear.
Some said it was because he had no wife,
And hated to be twitted on the subject;
Others because he'd come within a day
Or so of having one, and then been Jilted;
Others because he'd had one once, a good one,
Who'd run away with someone else and left him;
And others still because he had one now
He only had to be reminded of--
He was all duty to her in a minute:
He had to run right off to look her up,
As if to say, "That's so, how is my wife?
I hope she isn't getting into mischief."
No one was anxious to get rid of Paul.
He'd been the hero of the mountain camps
Ever since, just to show them, he had slipped
The bark of a whole tamarack off whole
As clean as boys do off a willow twig
To make a willow whistle on a Sunday
April by subsiding meadow brooks.
They seemed to ask him just to see him go,
"How is the wife, Paul?" and he always went.
He never stopped to murder anyone
Who asked the question. He just disappeared--

Nobody knew in what direction,
Although it wasn't usually long
Before they heard of him in some new camp,
The same Paul at the same old feats of logging.
The question everywhere was why should Paul
Object to being asked a civil question--
A man you could say almost anything to
Short of a fighting word. You have the answers.
And there was one more not so fair to Paul:
That Paul had married a wife not his equal.
Paul was ashamed of her. To match a hero
She would have had to be a heroine;
Instead of which she was some half-breed squaw.
But if the story Murphy told was true,
She wasn't anything to be ashamed of.

You know Paul could do wonders. Everyone's
Heard how he thrashed the horses on a load
That wouldn't budge, until they simply stretched
Their rawhide harness from the load to camp.
Paul told the boss the load would be all right,
"The sun will bring your load in"--and it did--
By shrinking the rawhide to natural length.
That's what is called a stretcher. But I guess
The one about his jumping so's to land
With both his feet at once against the ceiling,
And then land safely right side up again,
Back on the floor, is fact or pretty near fact.
Well, this is such a yarn. Paul sawed his wife
Out of a white-pine log. Murphy was there

And, as you might say, saw the lady born.
Paul worked at anything in lumbering.
He'd been hard at it taking boards away
For--I forget--the last ambitious sawyer
To want to find out if he couldn't pile
The lumber on Paul till Paul begged for mercy.
They'd sliced the first slab off a big butt log,
And the sawyer had slammed the carriage back
To slam end-on again against the saw teeth.
To judge them by the way they caught themselves
When they saw what had happened to the log,
They must have had a guilty expectation
Something was going to go with their slambanging.
Something had left a broad black streak of grease
On the new wood the whole length of the log
Except, perhaps, a foot at either end.
But when Paul put his finger in the grease,
It wasn't grease at all, but a long slot.
The log was hollow. They were sawing pine.
"First time I ever saw a hollow pine.
That comes of having Paul around the place.
Take it to bell for me," the sawyer said.
Everyone had to have a look at it
And tell Paul what he ought to do about it.
(They treated it as his.) "You take a jackknife,
And spread the opening, and you've got a dugout
All dug to go a-fishing in." To Paul
The hollow looked too sound and clean and empty
Ever to have housed birds or beasts or bees.
There was no entrance for them to get in by.

It looked to him like some new kind of hollow
He thought he'd better take his jackknife to.
So after work that evening be came back
And let enough light into it by cutting
To see if it was empty. He made out in there
A slender length of pith, or was it pith?
It might have been the skin a snake had cast
And left stood up on end inside the tree
The hundred years the tree must have been growing.
More cutting and he had this in both hands,
And looking from it to the pond nearby,
Paul wondered how it would respond to water.
Not a breeze stirred, but just the breath of air
He made in walking slowly to the beach
Blew it once off his hands and almost broke it.
He laid it at the edge, where it could drink.
At the first drink it rustled and grew limp.
At the next drink it grew invisible.
Paul dragged the shallows for it with his fingers,
And thought it must have melted. It was gone.
And then beyond the open water, dim with midges,
Where the log drive lay pressed against the boom,
It slowly rose a person, rose a girl,
Her wet hair heavy on her like a helmet,
Who, leaning on a log, looked back at Paul.
And that made Paul in turn look back
To see if it was anyone behind him
That she was looking at instead of him.
(Murphy had been there watching all the time,
But from a shed where neither of them could see him.)

There was a moment of suspense in birth
When the girl seemed too waterlogged to live,
Before she caught her first breath with a gasp
And laughed. Then she climbed slowly to her feet,
And walked off, talking to herself or Paul,
Across the logs like backs of alligators,
Paul taking after her around the pond.

Next evening Murphy and some other fellows
Got drunk, and tracked the pair up Catamount,
From the bare top of which there is a view
To other hills across a kettle valley.
And there, well after dark, let Murphy tell it,
They saw Paul and his creature keeping house.
It was the only glimpse that anyone
Has had of Paul and her since Murphy saw them
Falling in love across the twilight millpond.
More than a mile across the wilderness
They sat together halfway up a cliff
In a small niche let into it, the girl
Brightly, as if a star played on the place,
Paul darkly, like her shadow. All the light
Was from the girl herself, though, not from a star,
As was apparent from what happened next.
All those great ruffians put their throats together,
And let out a loud yell, and threw a bottle,
As a brute tribute of respect to beauty.
Of course the bottle fell short by a mile,
But the shout reached the girl and put her light out.
She went out like a firefly, and that was all.

So there were witnesses that Paul was married
And not to anyone to be ashamed of
Everyone had been wrong in judging Paul.
Murphy told me Paul put on all those airs
About his wife to keep her to himself.
Paul was what's called a terrible possessor.
Owning a wife with him meant owning her.
She wasn't anybody else's business,
Either to praise her or much as name her,
And he'd thank people not to think of her.
Murphy's idea was that a man like Paul
Wouldn't be spoken to about a wife
In any way the world knew how to speak.

NOTES

Another great one. They're all just wonderful. I love the sense of mystery. Why does he run off? I love the humor. There's all those great details. And I've mentioned I adore the saw mills. So the fact that sawing open lumber is involved is great as well.

It's sort of like discovering love in carving into marble, but now the love is found within a tree. Wood nymphs are real.

Luke MacNeil

Wild Grapes

What tree may not the fig be gathered from?
The grape may not be gathered from the birch?
It's all you know the grape, or know the birch.
As a girl gathered from the birch myself
Equally with my weight in grapes, one autumn,
I ought to know what tree the grape is fruit of.
I was born, I suppose, like anyone,
And grew to be a little boyish girl
My brother could not always leave at home.
But that beginning was wiped out in fear
The day I swung suspended with the grapes,
And was come after like Eurydice
And brought down safely from the upper regions;
And the life I live now's an extra life
I can waste as I please on whom I please.
So if you see me celebrate two birthdays,
And give myself out of two different ages,
One of them five years younger than I look-

One day my brother led me to a glade
Where a white birch he knew of stood alone,
Wearing a thin head-dress of pointed leaves,
And heavy on her heavy hair behind,
Against her neck, an ornament of grapes.
Grapes, I knew grapes from having seen them last year.
One bunch of them, and there began to be

Bunches all round me growing in white birches,
The way they grew round Leif the Lucky's German;
Mostly as much beyond my lifted hands, though,
As the moon used to seem when I was younger,
And only freely to be had for climbing.
My brother did the climbing; and at first
Threw me down grapes to miss and scatter
And have to hunt for in sweet fern and hardhack;
Which gave him some time to himself to eat,
But not so much, perhaps, as a boy needed.
So then, to make me wholly self-supporting,
He climbed still higher and bent the tree to earth
And put it in my hands to pick my own grapes.
"Here, take a tree-top, I'll get down another.
Hold on with all your might when I let go."
I said I had the tree. It wasn't true.
The opposite was true. The tree had me.
The minute it was left with me alone
It caught me up as if I were the fish
And it the fishpole. So I was translated
To loud cries from my brother of "Let go!
Don't you know anything, you girl? Let go!"
But I, with something of the baby grip
Acquired ancestrally in just such trees
When wilder mothers than our wildest now
Hung babies out on branches by the hands
To dry or wash or tan, I don't know which,
(You'll have to ask an evolutionist)-
I held on uncomplainingly for life.
My brother tried to make me laugh to help me.

"What are you doing up there in those grapes?
Don't be afraid. A few of them won't hurt you.
I mean, they won't pick you if you don't them."
Much danger of my picking anything!
By that time I was pretty well reduced
To a philosophy of hang-and-let-hang.
"Now you know how it feels," my brother said,
"To be a bunch of fox-grapes, as they call them,
That when it thinks it has escaped the fox
By growing where it shouldn't-on a birch,
Where a fox wouldn't think to look for it-
And if he looked and found it, couldn't reach it-
Just then come you and I to gather it.
Only you have the advantage of the grapes
In one way: you have one more stem to cling by,
And promise more resistance to the picker."

One by one I lost off my hat and shoes,
And still I clung. I let my head fall back,
And shut my eyes against the sun, my ears
Against my brother's nonsense; "Drop," he said,
"I'll catch you in my arms. It isn't far."
(Stated in lengths of him it might not be.)
"Drop or I'll shake the tree and shake you down."
Grim silence on my part as I sank lower,
My small wrists stretching till they showed the banjo strings.
"Why, if she isn't serious about it!
Hold tight awhile till I think what to do.
I'll bend the tree down and let you down by it."
I don't know much about the letting down;

But once I felt ground with my stocking feet
And the world came revolving back to me,
I know I looked long at my curled-up fingers,
Before I straightened them and brushed the bark off.
My brother said: "Don't you weigh anything?
Try to weigh something next time, so you won't
Be run off with by birch trees into space."

It wasn't my not weighing anything
So much as my not knowing anything-
My brother had been nearer right before.
I had not taken the first step in knowledge;
I had not learned to let go with the hands,
As still I have not learned to with the heart,
And have no wish to with the heart-nor need,
That I can see. The mind-is not the heart.
I may yet live, as I know others live,
To wish in vain to let go with the mind-
Of cares, at night, to sleep; but nothing tells me
That I need learn to let go with the heart.

NOTES

I love love love this one. Frost brings the kids to fresh life, and I certainly did my share of tree-climbing in birch, maple, and apple while growing up in Massachusetts. There were always things to climb. And of course I love the symbolism. The sense that one would grab on and hold tight just because it's what one does. It's my own philosophy. I hold on and will just plug on with things.

These aren't wild grapes; they're from a trip to a New Hampshire winery we like to visit.

Place for a Third

Nothing to say to all those marriages!
She had made three herself to three of his.
The score was even for them, three to three.
But come to die she found she cared so much:
She thought of children in a burial row;
Three children in a burial row were sad.
One man's three women in a burial row
Somehow made her impatient with the man.
And so she said to Laban, "You have done
A good deal right; don't do the last thing wrong.
Don't make me lie with those two other women."

Laban said, No, he would not make her lie
With anyone but that she had a mind to,
If that was how she felt, of course, he said.
She went her way. But Laban having caught
This glimpse of lingering person in Eliza,
And anxious to make all he could of it
With something he remembered in himself,
Tried to think how he could exceed his promise,
And give good measure to the dead, though thankless.
If that was how she felt, he kept repeating.
His first thought under pressure was a grave
In a new boughten grave plot by herself,
Under he didn't care how great a stone:
He'd sell a yoke of steers to pay for it.

And weren't there special cemetery flowers,
That, once grief sets to growing, grief may rest;
The flowers will go on with grief awhile,
And no one seem neglecting or neglected?
A prudent grief will not despise such aids.
He thought of evergreen and everlasting.
And then he had a thought worth many of these.
Somewhere must be the grave of the young boy
Who married her for playmate more than helpmate,
And sometimes laughed at what it was between them.
How would she like to sleep her last with him?
Where was his grave? Did Laban know his name?

He found the grave a town or two away,
The headstone cut with John, Beloved Husband,
Beside it room reserved; they say a sister's;
A never-married sister's of that husband,
Whether Eliza would be welcome there.
The dead was bound to silence: ask the sister.
So Laban saw the sister, and, saying nothing
Of where Eliza wanted not to lie,
And who had thought to lay her with her first love,
Begged simply for the grave. The sister's face
Fell all in wrinkles of responsibility.
She wanted to do right. She'd have to think.
Laban was old and poor, yet seemed to care;
And she was old and poor-but she cared, too.
They sat. She cast one dull, old look at him,
Then turned him out to go on other errands
She said he might attend to in the village,

While she made up her mind how much she cared-
And how much Laban cared-and why he cared,
(She made shrewd eyes to see where he came in.)

She'd looked Eliza up her second time,
A widow at her second husband's grave,
And offered her a home to rest awhile
Before she went the poor man's widow's way,
Housekeeping for the next man out of wedlock.
She and Eliza had been friends through all.
Who was she to judge marriage in a world
Whose Bible's so confused up in marriage counsel?
The sister had not come across this Laban;
A decent product of life's ironing-out;
She must not keep him waiting. Time would press
Between the death day and the funeral day.
So when she saw him coming in the street
She hurried her decision to be ready
To meet him with his answer at the door.
Laban had known about what it would be
From the way she had set her poor old mouth,
To do, as she had put it, what was right.

She gave it through the screen door closed between them:
"No, not with John. There wouldn't be no sense.
Eliza's had too many other men."

Laban was forced to fall back on his plan
To buy Eliza a plot to lie alone in:

Which gives him for himself a choice of lots
When his time comes to die and settle down.

NOTES

Frost is just so good at creating characters and situations. I could absolutely imagine locals around her in this sort of a situation. I've been in my share of local cemeteries in the course of various genealogical work. I've documented most of them around my own hometown of Sutton. I've been in a number of cemeteries in New Hampshire, helping a friend with her genealogy.

Two Witches

THE WITCH OF COOS

I stayed the night for shelter at a farm
Behind the mountain, with a mother and son,
Two old-believers. They did all the talking.

MOTHER. Folks think a witch who has familiar spirits
She could call up to pass a winter evening,
But won't, should be burned at the stake or something.
Summoning spirits isn't "Button, button,
Who's got the button," you're to understand.

SON. Mother can make a common table rear
And kick with two legs like an army mule.

MOTHER. And when I've done it, what good have I done?
Rather than tip a table for you, let me
Tell you what Ralle the Sioux Control once told me.
He said the dead had souls, but when I asked him
How that could be -- I thought the dead were souls,
He broke my trance. Don't that make you suspicious
That there's something the dead are keeping back?
Yes, there's something the dead are keeping back.

SON. You wouldn't want to tell him what we have

Up attic, mother?

MOTHER. Bones -- a skeleton.

SON. But the headboard of mother's bed is pushed
Against the attic door: the door is nailed.
It's harmless. Mother hears it in the night
Halting perplexed behind the barrier
Of door and headboard. Where it wants to get
Is back into the cellar where it came from.

MOTHER. We'll never let them, will we, son? We'll never!

SON. It left the cellar forty years ago
And carried itself like a pile of dishes
Up one flight from the cellar to the kitchen,
Another from the kitchen to the bedroom,
Another from the bedroom to the attic,
Right past both father and mother, and neither stopped it.
Father had gone upstairs; mother was downstairs.
I was a baby: I don't know where I was.

MOTHER. The only fault my husband found with me --
I went to sleep before I went to bed,
Especially in winter when the bed
Might just as well be ice and the clothes snow.
The night the bones came up the cellar-stairs
Toffile had gone to bed alone and left me,
But left an open door to cool the room off
So as to sort of turn me out of it.

I was just coming to myself enough
To wonder where the cold was coming from,
When I heard Toffile upstairs in the bedroom
And thought I heard him downstairs in the cellar.
The board we had laid down to walk dry-shod on
When there was water in the cellar in spring
Struck the hard cellar bottom. And then someone
Began the stairs, two footsteps for each step,
The way a man with one leg and a crutch,
Or little child, comes up. It wasn't Toffile:
It wasn't anyone who could be there.
The bulkhead double-doors were double-locked
And swollen tight and buried under snow.
The cellar windows were banked up with sawdust
And swollen tight and buried under snow.
It was the bones. I knew them -- and good reason.
My first impulse was to get to the knob
And hold the door. But the bones didn't try
The door; they halted helpless on the landing,
Waiting for things to happen in their favor.
The faintest restless rustling ran all through them.
I never could have done the thing I did
If the wish hadn't been too strong in me
To see how they were mounted for this walk.
I had a vision of them put together
Not like a man, but like a chandelier.
So suddenly I flung the door wide on him.
A moment he stood balancing with emotion,
And all but lost himself. (A tongue of fire
Flashed out and licked along his upper teeth.

Smoke rolled inside the sockets of his eyes.)
Then he came at me with one hand outstretched,
The way he did in life once; but this time
I struck the hand off brittle on the floor,
And fell back from him on the floor myself.
The finger-pieces slid in all directions.
(Where did I see one of those pieces lately?
Hand me my button-box -- it must be there.)
I sat up on the floor and shouted, "Toffile,
It's coming up to you." It had its choice
Of the door to the cellar or the hall.
It took the hall door for the novelty,
And set off briskly for so slow a thing,
Still going every which way in the joints, though,
So that it looked like lightning or a scribble,
From the slap I had just now given its hand.
I listened till it almost climbed the stairs
From the hall to the only finished bedroom,
Before I got up to do anything;
Then ran and shouted, "Shut the bedroom door,
Toffile, for my sake!" "Company?" he said,
"Don't make me get up; I'm too warm in bed."
So lying forward weakly on the handrail
I pushed myself upstairs, and in the light
(The kitchen had been dark) I had to own
I could see nothing. "Toffile, I don't see it.
It's with us in the room, though. It's the bones."
"What bones?" "The cellar bones -- out of the grave."
That made him throw his bare legs out of bed
And sit up by me and take hold of me.

I wanted to put out the light and see
If I could see it, or else mow the room,
With our arms at the level of our knees,
And bring the chalk-pile down. "I'll tell you what --
It's looking for another door to try.
The uncommonly deep snow has made him think
Of his old song, The Wild Colonial Boy,
He always used to sing along the tote road.
He's after an open door to get outdoors.
Let's trap him with an open door up attic."
Toffile agreed to that, and sure enough,
Almost the moment he was given an opening,
The steps began to climb the attic stairs.
I heard them. Toffile didn't seem to hear them.
"Quick!" I slammed to the door and held the knob.
"Toffile, get nails." I made him nail the door shut
And push the headboard of the bed against it.
Then we asked was there anything
Up attic that we'd ever want again.
The attic was less to us than the cellar.
If the bones liked the attic, let them like it.
Let them stay in the attic. When they sometimes
Come down the stairs at night and stand perplexed
Behind the door and headboard of the bed,
Brushing their chalky skull with chalky fingers,
With sounds like the dry rattling of a shutter,
That's what I sit up in the dark to say --
To no one any more since Toffile died.
Let them stay in the attic since they went there.
I promised Toffile to be cruel to them

For helping them be cruel once to him.

SON. We think they had a grave down in the cellar.

MOTHER. We know they had a grave down in the cellar.

SON. We never could find out whose bones they were.

MOTHER. Yes, we could too, son. Tell the truth for once.
They were a man's his father killed for me.
I mean a man he killed instead of me.
The least I could do was help dig their grave.
We were about it one night in the cellar.

Son knows the story: but 'twas not for him
To tell the truth, suppose the time had come.
Son looks surprised to see me end a lie
We'd kept up all these years between ourselves
So as to have it ready for outsiders.
But tonight I don't care enough to lie --
I don't remember why I ever cared.
Toffile, if he were here, I don't believe
Could tell you why he ever cared himself....

She hadn't found the finger-bone she wanted
Among the buttons poured out in her lap.
I verified the name next morning: Toffile.
The rural letter box said Toffile Lajway.

NOTES

There's a reason Frost won the Pulitzer Prize. The poems are just gems. All the details about the double doors being snowed in. Been there. Dealt with that. The board to handle the wet cellar floor. The way the identity of the bones slowly comes out.

When you stay in these creaky old houses in New England you would think every single one had skeletons lurking around in them …

Here's a traditional house in New Hampshire – Ocean Born Mary's.

THE PAUPER WITCH OF GRAFTON

Now that they've got it settled whose I be,
I'm going to tell them something they won't like:
They've got it settled wrong, and I can prove it.
Flattered I must be to have two towns fighting
To make a present of me to each other.
They don't dispose me, either one of them,
To spare them any trouble. Double trouble's
Always the witch's motto anyway.
I'll double theirs for both of them -- you watch me.
They'll find they've got the whole thing to do over,
That is, if facts is what they want to go by.
They set a lot (now don't they?) by a record
Of Arthur Amy's having once been up
For Hog Reeve in March Meeting here in Warren.

I could have told them any time this twelvemonth
The Arthur Amy I was married to
Couldn't have been the one they say was up
In Warren at March Meeting for the reason
He wa'n't but fifteen at the time they say.
The Arthur Amy I was married to
Voted the only times he ever voted,
Which wasn't many, in the town of Wentworth.
One of the times was when 'twas in the warrant
To see if the town wanted to take over
The tote road to our clearing where we lived.
I'll tell you who'd remember -- Heman Lapish.
Their Arthur Amy was the father of mine.

So now they've dragged it through the law courts once
I guess they'd better drag it through again.
Wentworth and Warren's both good towns to live in,
Only I happen to prefer to live
In Wentworth from now on; and when all's said,
Right's right, and the temptation to do right
When I can hurt someone by doing it
Has always been too much for me, it has.
I know of some folks that'd be set up
At having in their town a noted witch:
But most would have to think of the expense
That even I would be. They ought to know
That as a witch I'd often milk a bat
And that'd be enough to last for days.
It'd make my position stronger, think,
If I was to consent to give some sign
To make it surer that I was a witch?
It wa'n't no sign, I s'pose, when Mallice Huse
Said that I took him out in his old age
And rode all over everything on him
Until I'd had him worn to skin and bones,
And if I'd left him hitched unblanketed
In front of one Town Hall, I'd left him hitched
In front of every one in Grafton County.
Some cried shame on me not to blanket him,
The poor old man. It would have been all right
If someone hadn't said to gnaw the posts
He stood beside and leave his trade mark on them,
So they could recognize them. Not a post
That they could hear tell of was scarified.

They made him keep on gnawing till he whined.
Then that same smarty someone said to look --
He'd bet Huse was a cribber and had gnawed
The crib he slept in -- and as sure's you're born
They found he'd gnawed the four posts of his bed,
All four of them to splinters. What did that prove?
Not that he hadn't gnawed the hitching posts
He said he had besides. Because a horse
Gnaws in the stable ain't no proof to me
He don't gnaw trees and posts and fences too.
But everybody took it for a proof.
I was a strapping girl of twenty then.
The smarty someone who spoiled everything
Was Arthur Amy. You know who he was.
That was the way he started courting me.
He never said much after we were married,
But I mistrusted he was none too proud
Of having interfered in the Huse business.
I guess he found he got more out of me
By having me a witch. Or something happened
To turn him round. He got to saying things
To undo what he'd done and make it right,
Like, "No, she ain't come back from kiting yet.
Last night was one of her nights out. She's kiting.
She thinks when the wind makes a night of it
She might as well herself." But he liked best
To let on he was plagued to death with me:
If anyone had seen me coming home
Over the ridgepole, 'stride of a broomstick,
As often as he had in the tail of the night,

He guessed they'd know what he had to put up with.
Well, I showed Arthur Amy signs enough
Off from the house as far as we could keep
And from barn smells you can't wash out of plowed ground
With all the rain and snow of seven years;
And I don't mean just skulls of Rogers' Rangers
On Moosilauke, but woman signs to man,
Only bewitched so I would last him longer.
Up where the trees grow short, the mosses tall,
I made him gather me wet snow berries
On slippery rocks beside a waterfall.
I made him do it for me in the dark.
And he liked everything I made him do.
I hope if he is where he sees me now
He's so far off he can't see what I've come to.
You can come down from everything to nothing.
All is, if I'd a-known when I was young
And full of it, that this would be the end,
It doesn't seem as if I'd had the courage
To make so free and kick up in folks' faces.
I might have, but it doesn't seem as if.

NOTES

I live right near a town named Grafton in Massachusetts, but this Grafton, New Hampshire is up in the center of New Hampshire. The witch is a great character. You get the real sense of her being a spitfire and now realizing it's trickier as you age. You start to actually want some support from your community.

I'm a descendant of one of the Salem witches – my ancestor was dragged into jail and then died there. Which perhaps is better than being publicly squashed under stones or hung. Still, it's not a wonderful end for anyone. She only confessed to protect her daughter and granddaughter from harm.

An Empty Threat

I stay;
But it isn't as if
There wasn't always Hudson's Bay
And the fur trade,
A small skiff
And a paddle blade.

I can just see my tent pegged,
And me on the floor,
Cross-legged,
And a trapper looking in at the door
With furs to sell.

His name's Joe,
Alias John,
And between what he doesn't know
And won't tell
About where Henry Hudson's gone,
I can't say he's much help;
But we get on.

The seal yelp
On an ice cake.
It's not men by some mistake?
No,
There's not a soul

For a windbreak
Between me and the North Pole—

Except always John-Joe,
My French Indian Esquimaux,
And he's off setting traps
In one himself perhaps.

Give a headshake
Over so much bay
Thrown away
In snow and mist
That doesn't exist,

I was going to say,
For God, man, or beast's sake,
Yet does perhaps for all three.

Don't ask Joe
What it is to him.
It's sometimes dim
What it is to me,
Unless it be
It's the old captain's dark fate
Who failed to find or force a strait
In its two-thousand-mile coast;
And his crew left him where be failed,
And nothing came of all be sailed.

It's to say, 'You and I—'

To such a ghost—
You and I
Off here
With the dead race of the Great Auk!'
And, 'Better defeat almost,
If seen clear,
Than life's victories of doubt
That need endless talk-talk
To make them out.'

NOTES

There's just something about winter up here. Everything gets white, and flat, and so cold. There's a certain kind of person who hunkers down and endures. You have to just take a long breath and know you're going to get through until spring.

There are still plenty of hunters and trappers who live similar lives to those a hundred, two hundred years ago. And there's a great Native American museum in New Hampshire that provides all sorts of details about the ones who were here first.

Allison Nunn

A Fountain, a Bottle, a Donkey's Ears, and Some Books

Old Davis owned a solid mica mountain
In Dalton that would someday make his fortune.
There'd been some Boston people out to see it:
And experts said that deep down in the mountain
The mica sheets were big as plate-glass windows.
He'd like to take me there and show it to me.

"I'll tell you what you show me. You remember
You said you knew the place where once, on Kinsman,
The early Mormons made a settlement
And built a stone baptismal font outdoors—
But Smith, or someone, called them off the mountain
To go West to a worse fight with the desert.
You said you'd seen the stone baptismal font.
Well, take me there."

"Someday I will."

"Today."

"Huh, that old bathtub, what is that to see?
Let's talk about it."

"Let's go see the place."

"To shut you up I'll tell you what I'll do:
I'll find that fountain if it takes all summer,
And both of our united strengths, to do it."

"You've lost it, then?"

"Not so but I can find it.
No doubt it's grown up some to woods around it.
The mountain may have shifted since I saw it
In eighty-five."

"As long ago as that?"

"If I remember rightly, it had sprung
A leak and emptied then. And forty years
Can do a good deal to bad masonry.
You won't see any Mormon swimming in it.
But you have said it, and we're off to find it.
Old as I am, I'm going to let myself
Be dragged by you all over everywhere———"
"I thought you were a guide."

"I am a guide,
And that's why I can't decently refuse you."

We made a day of it out of the world,
Ascending to descend to reascend.
The old man seriously took his bearings,
And spoke his doubts in every open place.

We came out on a look-off where we faced
A cliff, and on the cliff a bottle painted,
Or stained by vegetation from above,
A likeness to surprise the thrilly tourist.

"Well, if I haven't brought you to the fountain,
At least I've brought you to the famous Bottle."

"I won't accept the substitute. It's empty."

"So's everything."

"I want my fountain."

"I guess you'd find the fountain just as empty.
And anyway this tells me where I am."

"Hadn't you long suspected where you were?"

"You mean miles from that Mormon settlement?
Look here, you treat your guide with due respect
If you don't want to spend the night outdoors.
I vow we must be near the place from where
The two converging slides, the avalanches,
On Marshall, look like donkey's ears.
We may as well see that and save the day."

"Don't donkey's ears suggest we shake our own?"

"For God's sake, aren't you fond of viewing nature?
You don't like nature. All you like is books.
What signify a donkey's cars and bottle,
However natural? Give you your books!
Well then, right here is where I show you books.
Come straight down off this mountain just as fast
As we can fall and keep a-bouncing on our feet.
It's hell for knees unless done hell-for-leather."

Be ready, I thought, for almost anything.

We struck a road I didn't recognize,
But welcomed for the chance to lave my shoes
In dust once more. We followed this a mile,
Perhaps, to where it ended at a house
I didn't know was there. It was the kind
To bring me to for broad-board paneling.
I never saw so good a house deserted.

"Excuse me if I ask you in a window
That happens to be broken", Davis said.
"The outside doors as yet have held against us.
I want to introduce you to the people
Who used to live here. They were Robinsons.
You must have heard of Clara Robinson,
The poetess who wrote the book of verses
And had it published. It was all about
The posies on her inner windowsill,
And the birds on her outer windowsill,
And how she tended both, or had them tended:

She never tended anything herself.
She was 'shut in' for life. She lived her whole
Life long in bed, and wrote her things in bed.
I'll show You how she had her sills extended
To entertain the birds and hold the flowers.
Our business first's up attic with her books."

We trod uncomfortably on crunching glass
Through a house stripped of everything
Except, it seemed, the poetess's poems.
Books, I should say!—-if books are what is needed.
A whole edition in a packing case
That, overflowing like a horn of plenty,
Or like the poetess's heart of love,
Had spilled them near the window, toward the light
Where driven rain had wet and swollen them.
Enough to stock a village library—
Unfortunately all of one kind, though.
They had been brought home from some publisher
And taken thus into the family.
Boys and bad hunters had known what to do
With stone and lead to unprotected glass:
Shatter it inward on the unswept floors.
How had the tender verse escaped their outrage?
By being invisible for what it was,
Or else by some remoteness that defied them
To find out what to do to hurt a poem.
Yet oh! the tempting flatness of a book,
To send it sailing out the attic window
Till it caught wind and, opening out its covers,

Tried to improve on sailing like a tile
By flying like a bird (silent in flight,
But all the burden of its body song),
Only to tumble like a stricken bird,
And lie in stones and bushes unretrieved.
Books were not thrown irreverently about.
They simply lay where someone now and then,
Having tried one, had dropped it at his feet
And left it lying where it fell rejected.
Here were all those the poetess's life
Had been too short to sell or give away.

"Take one," Old Davis bade me graciously.

"Why not take two or three?"

"Take all you want."
"Good-looking books like that." He picked one fresh
In virgin wrapper from deep in the box,
And stroked it with a horny-handed kindness.
He read in one and I read in another,
Both either looking for or finding something.

The attic wasps went missing by like bullets.

I was soon satisfied for the time being.

All the way home I kept remembering
The small book in my pocket. It was there.
The poetess had sighed, I knew, in heaven

At having eased her heart of one more copy—
Legitimately. My demand upon her,
Though slight, was a demand. She felt the tug.
In time she would be rid of all her books.

NOTES

Delightful details, are they going to find the fountain? Are they not? It twists and turns just like real adventures in the forests around here. You never know what you're going to find. And I love the idea that they find a box of books she never got around to selling. Most authors I know have a box or two of books in their house that they want to get sold.

Tina K. Brennan

I Will Sing You One-O

It was long I lay
Awake that night
Wishing that night
Would name the hour
And tell me whether
To call it day
(Though not yet light)
And give up sleep.
The snow fell deep
With the hiss of spray;
Two winds would meet,
One down one street,
One down another,
And fight in a smother
Of dust and feather.
I could not say,
But feared the cold
Had checked the pace
Of the tower clock
By tying together
Its hands of gold
Before its face.

Then came one knock!
A note unruffled
Of earthly weather,

Though strange and muffled.
The tower said, "One!'
And then a steeple.
They spoke to themselves
And such few people
As winds might rouse
From sleeping warm
(But not unhouse).
They left the storm
That struck en masse
My window glass
Like a beaded fur.
In that grave One
They spoke of the sun
And moon and stars,
Saturn and Mars
And Jupiter.
Still more unfettered,
They left the named
And spoke of the lettered,
The sigmas and taus
Of constellations.
They filled their throats
With the furthest bodies
To which man sends his
Speculation,
Beyond which God is;
The cosmic motes
Of yawning lenses.
Their solemn peals

Were not their own:
They spoke for the clock
With whose vast wheels
Theirs interlock.
In that grave word
Uttered alone
The utmost star
Trembled and stirred,
Though set so far
Its whirling frenzies
Appear like standing
in one self station.
It has not ranged,
And save for the wonder
Of once expanding
To be a nova,
It has not changed
To the eye of man
On planets over
Around and under
It in creation
Since man began
To drag down man
And nation nation.

NOTES

I remember those days, when I didn't have a lit clock by my bed. I'd wake up in the middle of the night and wonder just how late it was. Was dawn almost here? Was it worth just waking up? Or should I try to tough it out and get some more sleep?

I love how it brings in that sense of late night wonder, and the wheeling stars and planets.

Mount Washington is a classic place to explore the skies.

Fragmentary Blue

Why make so much of fragmentary blue
In here and there a bird, or butterfly,
Or flower, or wearing-stone, or open eye,
When heaven presents in sheets the solid hue?

Since earth is earth, perhaps, not heaven (as yet) –
Though some savants make earth include the sky;
And blue so far above us comes so high,
It only gives our wish for blue a whet.

NOTES

This is almost like a haiku, with how beautifully it presents the imagery. The skies around here do turn a brilliant blue, especially in the summertime. And it's true, when you have that giant blue sky all above, why do you still delight in seeking out forget-me-nots with their tiny blue flowers?

Tina K. Brennan

Fire and Ice

Some say the world will end in fire,
Some say in ice.
From what I've tasted of desire
I hold with those who favor fire.
But if it had to perish twice,
I think I know enough of hate
To say that for destruction ice
Is also great
And would suffice.

NOTES

This is one of the most famous poems from this book, probably because it's short and easily put on Pinterst or other similar online sites. It does have great power to it. We can all visualize that hot fire of passion. We can also feel the frigid ice of hatred.

Rumor has it that this poem influenced George R. R. Martin to start his series with *A Song of Fire and Ice*.

Luke MacNeil

In a Disused Graveyard

The living come with grassy tread
To read the gravestones on the hill;
The graveyard draws the living still,
But never anymore the dead.
The verses in it say and say:
"The ones who living come today
To read the stones and go away
Tomorrow dead will come to stay."
So sure of death the marbles rhyme,
Yet can't help marking all the time
How no one dead will seem to come.
What is it men are shrinking from?
It would be easy to be clever
And tell the stones: Men hate to die
And have stopped dying now forever.
I think they would believe the lie.

NOTES

A great vision and insight. I visit cemeteries a lot for genealogy and it's true – so many cemeteries are "caught in time" in that they are just the way they are. People come to take photos of the stones but nobody is being buried there any more. Sometimes it's because they are all being buried in a newer graveyard. Other times it's because so many people are being cremated or having other things done instead.

Dust of Snow

The way a crow
Shook down on me
The dust of snow
From a hemlock tree

Has given my heart
A change of mood
And saved some part
Of a day I had rued.

NOTES

This is another delightful haiku-type image. I've definitely had crows and squirrels shake down snow on me. I think they do it on purpose ☺. It does make you smile.

Tom Brooks

To E.T.

I slumbered with your poems on my breast
Spread open as I dropped them half-read through
Like dove wings on a figure on a tomb
To see, if in a dream they brought of you,

I might not have the chance I missed in life
Through some delay, and call you to your face
First solider, and then poet, and then both,
Who died a soldier-poet of your race.

I meant, you meant, that nothing should remain
Unsaid between us, brother, and this remained--
And one thing more that was not then to say:
The Victory for what it lost and gained.

You went to meet the shell's embrace of fire
On Vimy Ridge; and when you fell that day
The war seemed over more for you than me,
But now for me than you--the other way.

How ever, though, for even me who knew
The foe thrust back unsafe beyond the Rhine,
If I was not speak of it to you
And see you pleased once more with words of mine?

NOTES

This is a powerful, personal ode to Frost's good friend Edward Thomas. Frost met him in England. Frost had really wanted Edward to come live near him in New England, but Edward went to World War I instead – and he died there.

Tom Brooks

Nothing Gold Can Stay

Nature's first green is gold,
Her hardest hue to hold.
Her early leaf's a flower;
But only so an hour.
Then leaf subsides to leaf.
So Eden sank to grief,
So dawn goes down to day.
Nothing gold can stay.

NOTES

The Outsiders with a star-studded cast of actors came out in 1983 – I was a sophomore in high school so it was just about perfect timing. The "boys" in the movie were just the same age as the boys in my own school. I knew those challenges between the kids with money and the kids without. We had our own jeans-wearing outsiders and then the preppy rich kids with their own cars.

This poem featured prominently in the movie and in the base book. It portrays the theme of their innocence being lost.

I'd already liked Robert Frost before this, but the poem being so entwined in the movie just made it that much better.

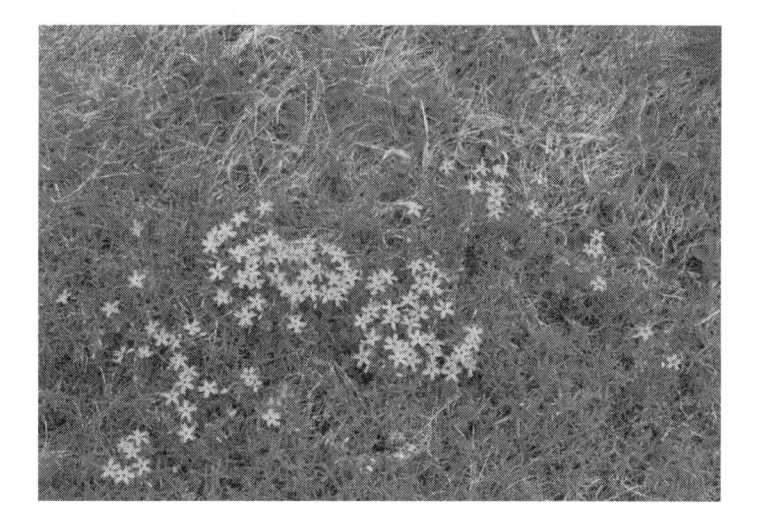

The Runaway

Once when the snow of the year was beginning to fall,
We stopped by a mountain pasture to say "Whose colt?"
A little Morgan had one forefoot on the wall,
The other curled at his breast. He dipped his head
And snorted at us. And then he had to bolt.
We heard the miniature thunder where he fled,
And we saw him, or thought we saw him, dim and grey,
Like a shadow against the curtain of falling flakes.
"I think the little fellow's afraid of the snow.
He isn't winter-broken. It isn't play
With the little fellow at all. He's running away.
I doubt if even his mother could tell him, 'Sakes,
It's only weather.' He'd think she didn't know!
Where is his mother? He can't be out alone."
And now he comes again with a clatter of stone
And mounts the wall again with whited eyes
And all his tail that isn't hair up straight.
He shudders his coat as if to throw off flies.
"Whoever it is that leaves him out so late,
When other creatures have gone to stall and bin,
Ought to be told to come and take him in."

NOTES

This is another one where you can really see it happening. Young animals are so cute to watch, as they discover the seasons and what they're all about!

Tom Brooks

The Aim Was Song

Before man came to blow it right
The wind once blew itself untaught,
And did its loudest day and night
In any rough place where it caught.

Man came to tell it what was wrong:
I hadn't found the place to blow;
It blew too hard--the aim was song.
And listen--how it ought to go!

He took a little in his mouth,
And held it long enough for north
To be converted into south,
And then by measure blew it forth.

By measure. It was word and note,
The wind the wind had meant to be--
A little through the lips and throat.
The aim was song--the wind could see.

NOTES

I like the images here, of wind blowing wildly and gently being taught a new trick. There are definitely all kinds of winds out here. Maybe it's the forests, or maybe it's the mountains. The wind makes a wild number of sounds. Of course, the old houses don't help with that, either.

And the absolute kind of the wind is Mount Washington.

Stopping by Woods on a Snowy Evening

Whose woods these are I think I know.
His house is in the village, though;
He will not see me stopping here
To watch his woods fill up with snow.

My little horse must think it queer
To stop without a farmhouse near
Between the woods and frozen lake
The darkest evening of the year.

He gives his harness bells a shake
To ask if there is some mistake.
The only other sound's the sweep
Of easy wind and downy flake.

The woods are lovely, dark and deep,
But I have promises to keep,
And miles to go before I sleep,
And miles to go before I sleep.

NOTES

This is the one. This is the one I have memorized and have written versions of and merrily quote as I'm walking around through snowy woods, looking for stone walls. It is just so lovely. I love the sound of snow falling in the winter. I love the gentle sound of the wind.

And Frost of course adds on the layers of meaning, about a journey through life.

Luke MacNeil

For Once, Then, Something

Others taught me with having knelt at well-curbs
Always wrong to the light, so never seeing
Deeper down in the well than where the water
Gives me back in a shining surface picture
Me myself in the summer heaven godlike
Looking out of a wreath of fern and cloud puffs.
Once, when trying with chin against a well-curb,
I discerned, as I thought, beyond the picture,
Through the picture, a something white, uncertain,
Something more of the depths--and then I lost it.
Water came to rebuke the too clear water.
One drop fell from a fern, and lo, a ripple
Shook whatever it was lay there at bottom,
Blurred it, blotted it out. What was that whiteness?
Truth? A pebble of quartz? For once, then, something.

NOTES

Another haiku-like moment. I've definitely had those moments where I tried to see deeper into a pool of water, to see what's down beneath that surface. If the sun's hitting it like that, it can be nearly impossible. And it's like there's an entire other world down there.

Tom Brooks

Blue-Butterfly Day

It is blue-butterfly day here in spring,
And with these sky-flakes down in flurry on flurry
There is more unmixed color on the wing
Than flowers will show for days unless they hurry.

But these are flowers that fly and all but sing:
And now from having ridden out desire
They lie closed over in the wind and cling
Where wheels have freshly sliced the April mire.

NOTES

This poem is also a haiku-like one but for some reason it doesn't grab me as strongly as many others. Maybe because here in Massachusetts we do have large orange butterflies but we don't have flocks of little blue butterflies. So the imagery of a flock of little blue butterflies in spring doesn't really resonate for me.

Still, I do appreciate it. And the thought that first they are fluttering around and then they come to rest their wings in muddy tire tracks.

The Onset

Always the same, when on a fated night
At last the gathered snow lets down as white
As may be in dark woods, and with a song
It shall not make again all winter long
Of hissing on the yet uncovered ground,
I almost stumble looking up and round,
As one who overtaken by the end
Gives up his errand, and lets death descend
Upon him where he is, with nothing done
To evil, no important triumph won,
More than if life had never been begun.

Yet all the precedent is on my side:
I know that winter death has never tried
The earth but it has failed: the snow may heap
In long storms an undrifted four feet deep
As measured again maple, birch, and oak,
It cannot check the peeper's silver croak;
And I shall see the snow all go down hill
In water of a slender April rill
That flashes tail through last year's withered brake
And dead weeds, like a disappearing snake.
Nothing will be left white but here a birch,
And there a clump of houses with a church.

NOTES

I love all the seasons here in New England. Winter is definitely magical. I always wait for that first real snow. The beautiful white fluffiness.

I love all the details here. How you wait for that first layer to cover the ground. How it's special and new.

To Earthward

Love at the lips was touch
As sweet as I could bear;
And once that seemed too much;
I lived on air

That crossed me from sweet things,
The scent of -- was it musk
From hidden grapevine springs
Down hill at dusk?

I had the swirl and ache
From sprays of honeysuckle
That when they're gathered shake
Dew on the knuckle.

I craved sweet things, but those
Seemed strong when I was young;
The petal of the rose
It was that stung.

Now no joy but lacks salt
That is not dashed with pain

And weariness and fault;
I crave the stain

Of tears, the aftermark
Of almost too much love,
The sweet of bitter bark
And burning clove.

When stiff and sore and scarred
I take away my hand
From leaning on it hard
In grass and sand,

The hurt is not enough:
I long for weight and strength
To feel the earth as rough
To all my length.

NOTES

This is one of Frost's clearer metaphorical sequences. We start with the young, sweet love and move along to the more settled adult love. And at the end he's ready for the next stage. To be in the earth.

Tom Brooks

Good-by and Keep Cold

This saying good-by on the edge of the dark
And the cold to an orchard so young in the bark
Reminds me of all that can happen to harm
An orchard away at the end of the farm
All winter, cut off by a hill from the house.
I don't want it girdled by rabbit and mouse,
I don't want it dreamily nibbled for browse
By deer, and I don't want it budded by grouse.
(If certain it wouldn't be idle to call
I'd summon grouse, rabbit, and deer to the wall
And warn them away with a stick for a gun.)
I don't want it stirred by the heat of the sun.
(We made it secure against being, I hope,
By setting it out on a northerly slope.)
No orchard's the worse for the wintriest storm;
But one thing about it, it mustn't get warm.
'How often already you've had to be told,
Keep cold, young orchard. Good-by and keep cold.
Dread fifty above more than fifty below.'
I have to be gone for a season or so.
My business awhile is with different trees,
less carefully nurtured, less fruitful than these,
And such as is done to their wood with an ax--
Maples and birches and tamaracks.
I wish I could promise to lie in the night
And think of an orchard's arboreal plight

When slowly (and nobody comes with a light)
Its heart sinks lower under the sod.
But something has to be left to God.

NOTES

There's an art to managing orchards in New England in the winter. Season after season we hear about the apple blossoms getting harmed by a late frost or by other thing happening in the winter to interfere. There is only so much we can do. You have to just pray sometimes.

You definitely get the sense here. He really needs the weather to behave for him.

Two Look at Two

Love and forgetting might have carried them
A little further up the mountain side
With night so near, but not much further up.
They must have halted soon in any case
With thoughts of a path back, how rough it was
With rock and washout, and unsafe in darkness;
When they were halted by a tumbled wall
With barbed-wire binding. They stood facing this,
Spending what onward impulse they still had
In One last look the way they must not go,
On up the failing path, where, if a stone
Or earthslide moved at night, it moved itself;
No footstep moved it. "This is all," they sighed,
"Good-night to woods." But not so; there was more.
A doe from round a spruce stood looking at them
Across the wall, as near the wall as they.
She saw them in their field, they her in hers.
The difficulty of seeing what stood still,
Like some up-ended boulder split in two,
Was in her clouded eyes; they saw no fear there.
She seemed to think that two thus they were safe.
Then, as if they were something that, though strange,
She could not trouble her mind with too long,
She sighed and passed unscared along the wall.
"This, then, is all. What more is there to ask?"
But no, not yet. A snort to bid them wait.

A buck from round the spruce stood looking at them
Across the wall as near the wall as they.
This was an antlered buck of lusty nostril,
Not the same doe come back into her place.
He viewed them quizzically with jerks of head,
As if to ask, "Why don't you make some motion?
Or give some sign of life? Because you can't.
I doubt if you're as living as you look."
Thus till he had them almost feeling dared
To stretch a proffering hand -- and a spell-breaking.
Then he too passed unscared along the wall.
Two had seen two, whichever side you spoke from.
"This must be all." It was all. Still they stood,
A great wave from it going over them,
As if the earth in one unlooked-for favour
Had made them certain earth returned their love.

NOTES

This is the beauty of rural paths around New Hampshire and Massachusetts. You come across turkey, deer, and all sorts of other things. If you are calm and peaceful, the animals tend to be relaxed as well.

A lovely portrayal of a special moment.

Not to Keep

They sent him back to her. The letter came
Saying... And she could have him. And before
She could be sure there was no hidden ill
Under the formal writing, he was in her sight,
Living. They gave him back to her alive
How else? They are not known to send the dead
And not disfigured visibly. His face?
His hands? She had to look, and ask,
"What was it, dear?" And she had given all
And still she had all they had they the lucky!
Wasn't she glad now? Everything seemed won,
And all the rest for them permissible ease.
She had to ask, "What was it, dear?"

"Enough,
Yet not enough. A bullet through and through,
High in the breast. Nothing but what good care
And medicine and rest, and you a week,
Can cure me of to go again." The same
Grim giving to do over for them both.
She dared no more than ask him with her eyes
How was it with him for a second trial.
And with his eyes he asked her not to ask.
They had given him back to her, but not to keep.

NOTES

Frost lost good friends in World War I – he knew the trauma that the war had caused. In this poem he touches on how it impacted the loved ones at home. A soldier has come home from war – but he wants to go right back again. His brothers in arm are fighting without him, and he can't just abandon them.

A Brook in the City

The firm house lingers, though averse to square
With the new city street it has to wear A number in.
But what about the brook
That held the house as in an elbow-crook?
I ask as one who knew the brook, its strength
And impulse, having dipped a finger length
And made it leap my knuckle, having tossed
A flower to try its currents where they crossed.
The meadow grass could be cemented down
From growing under pavements of a town;
The apple trees be sent to hearth-stone flame.
Is water wood to serve a brook the same?
How else dispose of an immortal force
No longer needed? Staunch it at its source
With cinder loads dumped down? The brook was
thrown Deep in a sewer dungeon under stone
In fetid darkness still to live and run -
And all for nothing it had ever done
Except forget to go in fear perhaps.
No one would know except for ancient maps
That such a brook ran water. But I wonder
If from its being kept forever under
The thoughts may not have risen that so keep
This new-built city from both work and sleep.

NOTES

This is a powerful one for me because in the Blackstone Valley they used to have a canal which ran from Worcester, MA to Providence, RI. It was a huge engineering feat to create this canal. And then just a decade or two later, the railroad came in, and soon the entire canal was being bypassed. They covered it all back up and now it's used for sewers.

The Kitchen Chimney

Builder, in building the little house,
In every way you may please yourself;
But please please me in the kitchen chimney:
Don't build me a chimney upon a shelf.

However far you must go for bricks,
Whatever they cost a-piece or a pound,
Buy me enough for a full-length chimney,
And build the chimney clear from the ground.

It's not that I'm greatly afraid of fire,
But I never heard of a house that throve
(And I know of one that didn't thrive)
Where the chimney started above the stove.

And I dread the ominous stain of tar
That there always is on the papered walls,
And the smell of fire drowned in rain
That there always is when the chimney's false.

A shelf's for a clock or vase or picture,
But I don't see why it should have to bear
A chimney that only would serve to remind me
Of castles I used to build in air.

NOTES

It might seem silly to care this much about how a chimney is built, but I know lots of people around here who do care about how this is done. Chimneys are such a key to getting through the long winters – we want it to be right.

Looking for a Sunset Bird in Winter

The west was getting out of gold,
The breath of air had died of cold,
When shoeing home across the white,
I thought I saw a bird alight.

In summer when I passed the place
I had to stop and lift my face;
A bird with an angelic gift
Was singing in it sweet and swift.

No bird was singing in it now.
A single leaf was on a bough,
And that was all there was to see
In going twice around the tree.

From my advantage on a hill
I judged that such a crystal chill
Was only adding frost to snow
As gilt to gold that wouldn't show.

A brush had left a crooked stroke
Of what was either cloud or smoke
From north to south across the blue;
A piercing little star was through.

NOTES

Winter is such an amazing season here in New Hampshire and New England. I've seen those squiggles in the sky. The glistening stars. The traceries of frost on snow. It's all captured here.

A Boundless Moment

He halted in the wind, and--what was that
Far in the maples, pale, but not a ghost?
He stood there bringing March against his thought,
And yet too ready to believe the most.

"Oh, that's the Paradise-in-bloom," I said;
And truly it was fair enough for flowers
had we but in us to assume in March
Such white luxuriance of May for ours.

We stood a moment so in a strange world,
Myself as one his own pretense deceives;
And then I said the truth (and we moved on).
A young beech clinging to its last year's leaves.

NOTES

I've definitely had these sensations before – the wondering if spring was coming early this year. And then you realize that no, winter is still going to linger on a bit more.

Evening in a Sugar Orchard

From where I lingered in a lull in March
outside the sugar-house one night for choice,
I called the fireman with a careful voice
And bade him leave the pan and stoke the arch:
'O fireman, give the fire another stoke,
And send more sparks up chimney with the smoke.'
I thought a few might tangle, as they did,
Among bare maple boughs, and in the rare
Hill atmosphere not cease to glow,
And so be added to the moon up there.
The moon, though slight, was moon enough to show
On every tree a bucket with a lid,
And on black ground a bear-skin rug of snow.
The sparks made no attempt to be the moon.
They were content to figure in the trees
As Leo, Orion, and the Pleiades.
And that was what the boughs were full of soon.

NOTES

I love the imagery of the sparks in trees. So many trees around here have those buckets – we even have some in our own yard. The poem person is creating their own constellations with those sparks.

Gathering Leaves

Spades take up leaves
No better than spoons,
And bags full of leaves
Are light as balloons.

I make a great noise
Of rustling all day
Like rabbit and deer
Running away.

But the mountains I raise
Elude my embrace,
Flowing over my arms
And into my face.

I may load and unload
Again and again
Till I fill the whole shed,
And what have I then?

Next to nothing for weight,
And since they grew duller
From contact with earth,
Next to nothing for color.

Next to nothing for use.

But a crop is a crop,
And who's to say where
The harvest shall stop?

NOTES

Autumn leaves. One of the best things about living in this region is the beautiful autumn leaves for jumping in, piling up, and having fun with. I appreciate the person's desire to stick them all in a shed, but we just put them into compost bins ☺.

The Valley's Singing Day

The sound of the closing outside door was all.
You made no sound in the grass with your footfall,
As far as you went from the door, which was not far;
But had awakened under the morning star
The first song-bird that awakened all the rest.
He could have slept but a moment more at best.
Already determined dawn began to lay
In place across a cloud the slender ray
For prying beneath and forcing the lids of sight,
And loosing the pent-up music of over-night.
But dawn was not to begin their 'pearly-pearly';
(By which they mean the rain is pearls so early,
Before it changes to diamonds in the sun),
Neither was song that day to be self-begun.
You had begun it, and if there needed proof--
I was asleep still under the dripping roof,
My window curtain hung over the sill to wet;
But I should awake to confirm your story yet;
I should be willing to say and help you say
That once you had opened the valley's singing day.

NOTES

I'm more a night owl than a morning bird. Still, there have been those times that I'm up early and treasure that dew, the just-waking birds, and all the other beauty.

Misgiving

All crying, "We will go with you, O Wind!"
The foliage follow him, leaf and stem;
But a sleep oppresses them as they go,
And they end by bidding him stay with them.

Since ever they flung abroad in spring
The leaves had promised themselves this flight,
Who now would fain seek sheltering wall,
Or thicket, or hollow place for the night.

And now they answer his summoning blast
With an ever vaguer and vaguer stir,
Or at utmost a little reluctant whirl
That drops them no further than where they were.

I only hope that when I am free
As they are free to go in quest
Of the knowledge beyond the bounds of life
It may not seem better to me to rest.

NOTES

A great, powerful poem. First, anyone who lives up here is well familiar with the way autumn leaves fall, swirl, whirl, and dance. It's beautiful. Stunning. And as he does in so many places, Frost brings it to delightful life.

Then you mix in the underlying meaning of death. When we are finally freed in death, will we whirl and reach? Or will we just want to rest still, because we've lost all energy to do anything else ...

A Hillside Thaw

To think to know the country and not know
The hillside on the day the sun lets go
Ten million silver lizards out of snow!
As often as I've seen it done before
I can't pretend to tell the way it's done.
It looks as if some magic of the sun
Lifted the rug that bred them on the floor
And the light breaking on them made them run.
But if I thought to stop the wet stampede,
And caught one silver lizard by the tail,
And put my foot on one without avail,
And threw myself wet-elbowed and wet-kneed
In front of twenty others' wriggling speed,--
In the confusion of them all aglitter,
And birds that joined in the excited fun
By doubling and redoubling song and twitter,
I have no doubt I'd end by holding none.

It takes the moon for this. The sun's a wizard
By all I tell; but so's the moon a witch.
From the high west she makes a gentle cast
And suddenly, without a jerk or twitch,
She has her spell on every single lizard.
I fancied when I looked at six o'clock
The swarm still ran and scuttled just as fast.
The moon was waiting for her chill effect.

I looked at nine: the swarm was turned to rock
In every lifelike posture of the swarm,
Transfixed on mountain slopes almost erect.
Across each other and side by side they lay.
The spell that so could hold them as they were
Was wrought through trees without a breath of storm
To make a leaf, if there had been one, stir.
One lizard at the end of every ray.
The thought of my attempting such a stay!

NOTES

This poem, when found on the internet, usually is shown with several typos which change the meaning of the lines. It's a shame that those internet posters seem to just copy from each other without even checking the source material to see if it's accurate.

I've never seen a swarm of lizards like this, so this is fascinating. Frost is opening up a new world. And of course he has layers of meaning here, about how the sun and moon work in tandem, about how the world is always changing. We have to appreciate the now that we have.

Plowmen

A plow, they say, to plow the snow.
They cannot mean to plant it, no--
Unless in bitterness to mock
At having cultivated rock.

NOTES

This is like a delightful haiku – it brings to mind such vivid images! We in New England are well known for farming rocks. It seems no matter what type of farmland or garden you have that oodles of rocks grow like magic.

It's no wonder that anybody thinking of the word 'plow' would think of bringing up rocks. And it's fun to play with the idea of the plow for a snow vs the plow for your garden.

On a Tree Fallen Across the Road

(To hear us talk)

The tree the tempest with a crash of wood
Throws down in front of us is not bar
Our passage to our journey's end for good,
But just to ask us who we think we are

Insisting always on our own way so.
She likes to halt us in our runner tracks,
And make us get down in a foot of snow
Debating what to do without an ax.

And yet she knows obstruction is in vain:
We will not be put off the final goal
We have it hidden in us to attain,
Not though we have to seize earth by the pole

And, tired of aimless circling in one place,
Steer straight off after something into space.

NOTES

Yup, another part of living in New England. Trees come down. All. The. Time. You're just grateful when they don't take out your car or your roof. Trees in roads? That's just normal. You haul them out of the way if you can.

I like the idea that one has to take these hurdles as a normal part of life and just figure them out. It doesn't make sense to get upset by them.

Our Singing Strength

It snowed in spring on earth so dry and warm
The flakes could find no landing place to form.
Hordes spent themselves to make it wet and cold,
And still they failed of any lasting hold.
They made no white impression on the black.
They disappeared as if earth sent them back.
Not till from separate flakes they changed at night
To almost strips and tapes of ragged white
Did grass and garden ground confess it snowed,
And all go back to winter but the road.
Next day the scene was piled and puffed and dead.
The grass lay flattened under one great tread.
Borne down until the end almost took root,
The rangey bough anticipated fruit
With snowball cupped in every opening bud.
The road alone maintained itself in mud,
Whatever its secret was of greater heat
From inward fires or brush of passing feet.

In spring more mortal singers than belong
To any one place cover us with song.
Thrush, bluebird, blackbird, sparrow, and robin throng;
Some to go further north to Hudson's Bay,
Some that have come too far north back away,
Really a very few to build and stay.
Now was seen how these liked belated snow.
the field had nowhere left for them to go;
They'd soon exhausted all there was in flying;

The trees they'd had enough of with once trying
And setting off their heavy powder load.
They could find nothing open but the road.
So there they let their lives be narrowed in
By thousands the bad weather made akin.
The road became a channel running flocks
Of glossy birds like ripples over rocks.
I drove them under foot in bits of flight
That kept the ground, almost disputing right
Of way with me from apathy of wing,
A talking twitter all they had to sing.
A few I must have driven to despair
Made quick asides, but having done in air
A whir among white branches great and small
As in some too much carven marble hall
Where one false wing beat would have brought down all,
Came tamely back in front of me, the Drover,
To suffer the same driven nightmare over.
One such storm in a lifetime couldn't teach them
That back behind pursuit it couldn't reach them;
None flew behind me to be left alone.

Well, something for a snowstorm to have shown
The country's singing strength thus brought together,
the thought repressed and moody with the weather
Was none the less there ready to be freed
And sing the wildflowers up from root and seed.

NOTES

One of his longer ones, this lays out an interesting scene of exhausted birds all huddling together out of necessity in the road – one of the only places safe for them to land and hunker down. I haven't seen that happen so it must have been a fairly unusual sight. He captured it for us all to enjoy.

And also, of course, the layers of meaning about how adversity can draw us together and help us put aside differences.

The Lockless Door

It went many years,
But at last came a knock,
And I thought of the door
With no lock to lock.

I blew out the light,
I tip-toed the floor,
And raised both hands
In prayer to the door.

But the knock came again.
My window was wide;
I climbed on the sill
And descended outside.

Back over the sill
I bade a 'Come in'
To whatever the knock
At the door may have been.

So at a knock
I emptied my cage
To hide in the world
And alter with age.

NOTES

Like many of Frost's poems, this is based on a true event. He really was staying in a cottage and really did get so spooked by a knock that he climbed out the window. It turns out it was just a neighbor.

He's pointing out that often we are so afraid of what is coming that we take even more dangerous risks just to hide out from it.

The Need of Being Versed in Country Things

The house had gone to bring again
To the midnight sky a sunset glow.
Now the chimney was all of the house that stood,
Like a pistil after the petals go.

The barn opposed across the way,
That would have joined the house in flame
Had it been the will of the wind, was left
To bear forsaken the place's name.

No more it opened with all one end
For teams that came by the stony road
To drum on the floor with scurrying hoofs
And brush the mow with the summer load.

And birds that came to it through the air
At broken windows flew out and in.
Their murmur more like the sigh we sigh
From too much dwelling on what has been.

Yet for them the lilac renewed its leaf,
And the aged elm, though touched with fire;
And the dry pump flung up an awkward arm;

And the fence post carried a strand of wire.

For them there was really nothing sad.
But though they rejoiced in the nest they kept,
One had to be versed in country things
Not to believe the phoebes wept.

NOTES

The perfect way to end the book. I've seen these burned-down homes myself, just the chimney standing. And phoebes nest in our eaves, returning every year.

Life is about change. Nothing stays forever. They are just milestones we go past. The phoebes simply enjoy having somewhere to build their nest. They don't mind that sometimes they have to find a new location. It's just part of the progression of life.

Summary

Robert Frost just has a wonderful way with words. I adore his poetry and am so grateful this collection is finally in the public domain. There are so many websites out there with egregious typos in his poems. At least now people can read what he really wrote!

If you're able to take a trip to New Hampshire, to read them in their native environment, I highly recommend it!

Thank you for reading *New Hampshire*!

If you enjoyed this presentation, please leave feedback. All author's proceeds from this book benefit local arts programs. Together we can help make a difference!

If you're curious about any of my Holga photos, just let me know. I'm happy to explain how I took them. None of them are Photoshopped - they are all actual photos.

Be sure to sign up for my free newsletter! You'll get alerts of free books, discounts, and new releases. I run my own newsletter server – nobody else will ever see your email address. I promise!

http://www.lisashea.com/lisabase/subscribe.html

Please visit the following pages for news about free books, discounted releases, and new launches. Feel free to post questions there – I strive to answer within a day!

Facebook:

https://www.facebook.com/LisaSheaAuthor

Twitter:

https://twitter.com/LisaSheaAuthor

Google+:

https://plus.google.com/+LisaSheaAuthor/posts

Blog:

http://www.lisashea.com/lisabase/blog/

Share the news – we all want to enjoy interesting novels!

Dedication

To the Sutton Writing Group and Boston Writer's Group, which support me in all my writing quests.

Most of all, to my loyal fans who support me on Goodreads, Facebook, Twitter, and other platforms. It's because of you that I keep writing!

About the Author

I've been writing poetry and creating art since I was quite young. Robert Frost was always one of my favorite poems. The Snowy Woods poem, especially, really spoke to me. I love its imagery and rhythm.

I've published over 300 books in a variety of fiction and non-fiction genres.

Namaste.

Free Ebooks

All of the following ebooks should be available free on all platforms.

167

ARIES
An Adventurous Tale of Mythology and Folklore
1
Zodiac Maidens of Melk Short Stories
LISA SHEA

THE
COUNTERFEIT
LIGHTHOUSE
LISA SHEA

The
Proposal
A Romantic Short Story
Book 1 - NYC
LISA SHEA

BLACK SEA
DELUGE
A FLOOD MYTH SHORT STORY
1
LISA SHEA
The Historic Noah Flood Series

CHARTREUSE
A Sci-Fi
Short Story
Chartreuse -
a secret recipe from 1605 for
the Elixir of Long Life
LISA SHEA

DEATH
WATCH
A HORROR SHORT STORY
LISA SHEA

YOGA for
Stress Relief
and Forgiveness
Lisa Shea

Ten Minute
YOGA
for Stress Relief,
Focus,
and Renewal
Lisa Shea

YOGA
in Bed for All Ages
Start your day or
Prepare for sleep with
Calm relaxation
and serenity
Lisa Shea

YOGA for Traveling by Plane Train Bus & Car
Enjoy your Trip Relaxed, Serene & Energized!
Lisa Shea

JOURNALING BASICS
JOURNAL WRITING FOR BEGINNERS
LISA SHEA

Writing a VISION STATEMENT and SETTING GOALS
step by step techniques for reaching your dreams
LISA SHEA

Five Minute MEDITATION
Mindfulness, Stress Relief, and Focus for Absolute Beginners
LISA SHEA

CHAKRAS
In Yoga, Meditation, and Stress Relief
Lisa Shea

MEMORY Brain Training
Improve your Focus, Concentration, and Recall
Book 1: Amusement Parks
LISA SHEA

I may have added more free books since releasing this list here. For the most up to date version, be sure to visit:

http://www.lisashea.com/freebooks/

Thank you for supporting the cause!

Be the change you wish to see in the world.

Made in the USA
Columbia, SC
02 June 2025